The COMPLETE CROSS-STITCH

Other Books by the Author

Thelma R. Newman

Innovative Printmaking
Creative Candlemaking
Contemporary Decoupage
Contemporary African Arts and Crafts
Contemporary Southeast Asian Arts and Crafts
The Complete Book of Making Miniatures
Quilting, Patchwork, Appliqué, and Trapunto
Leather as Art and Craft
Crafting with Plastics
Plastics as an Art Form
Plastics as Design Form
Plastics as Sculpture
Woodcraft
Wax as Art Form

With Jay Hartley Newman

The Container Book

With Jay Hartley Newman and Lee Scott Newman

The Frame Book
The Lamp and Lighting Book
Paper as Art and Craft

The COMPLETE ROSS-STITCH

52 Stitches
in Embroidery and Gros Point
in New and Traditional
Designs and Methods

THELMA R. NEWMAN

Crown Publishers, Inc., New York

To Brandt Aymar, editor extraordinaire

Designed by Jon M. Nelson

Library of Congress Cataloging in Publication Data

. Newman, Thelma R
　　The complete cross-stitch.

　　Bibliography: p.
　　Includes index.
　　1.　Cross-stitch.　2.　Cross-stitch—Patterns.
I.　Title.
TT778.C76N48　1978　　746.4'4　　77-25237
ISBN 0-517-52839-8
ISBN 0-517-52840-1 pbk.

All photographs by the author or Lee Scott Newman,
unless otherwise noted.

Contents

Acknowledgments

My debts to creative people are far ranging. Anonymous craftspeople throughout the world have contributed the fruits of their traditions and skills to this book.

More specifically, I would like to express my endless love and appreciation to my sons Jay and Lee who helped work out and execute some designs for this book—to Lee for help with photographing and to Jay for checking and editing. I also appreciate Ginnie Thompson's contributions. These are duly noted.

Very special appreciation goes to Ann Reilly who fastidiously and skillfully diagrammed the charts for this book. She also helped program the step-by-step instructions for creating the many cross-stitches.

Thanks also to Gal Saturday Pat Weidner, and to Norm Smith for his very special photo processing.

And to husband Jack, the man behind the scenes, gratitude for facilitating so very much.

Thelma R. Newman

Preface

Embroidery was my first love. I still have an example that I had embroidered when I was four years old. The memory of my doing it is very clear after all these years. It is a doll's pinafore—a bit faded now but a testament to the ability of tiny fingers to wield a needle skillfully. I have been embroidering and collecting embroideries ever since.

There is something very relaxing and very satisfying about needlework. Perhaps it's the creative aspect of starting with a blank fabric or canvas and, by stitching colors of threads, producing a handsome surface that will last for many lifetimes. (I make things for those I love—for them to enjoy and to remember me by—a bit of immortality.)

It is hoped that some of the old and some of the new described and charted within this book will inspire and motivate you to create beautiful needlework. At the very least, even if you insert your own colors, something of you will be expressed. If every single act of creating a particular piece is not described, it is because it is my wish that you interpret and in the end express yourself. Inventions and those satisfying serendipitous events happen that way.

In this age of mechanization, needlework is not only a link with the past but also an activity for today—particularly when watching TV or riding on train or plane—and a gift for the future. There are some innovations here that utilize the latest of technology. In every case, the act of embroidery is one of creative enjoyment and is totally satisfying. I hope you agree.

Thelma R. Newman

Ethnic embroidered designs with cross-stitch on costumes date back hundreds of years and are seen all over the world. This is "Gaza" dress, interpreted by Margie Cloutier for Folkwear Patterns. Photo by Jerry Wainwright. Courtesy: Folkwear Patterns.

1 The Ubiquitous Cross-Stitch

ORIGINS

There has always been a reverence for embroidered work—particularly for the ubiquitous cross-stitch. The first cross-stitches probably appeared when x's were used to whip together animal skins. Inspiration for use of decorative cross-stitches was also just a short hop from the surface design of baskets that often contained crosses.

Ancient examples of cross-stitch embroidery have been discovered in China and Egypt (particularly from the Coptic period*) in the survival of fragile burial cloth and in embroidered patterns from paintings of the day. Bronze needles were found in the Indus Valley of India dating back to 2000 B.C.

Transmission of cross-stitch designs probably traveled as other skills had via trade routes through China and India to Afghanistan, Persia, Turkey (Thrace), Greece, and ancient Rome. And on another continent, fine examples embroidered at least 2,500 years ago by the Paracas were found in Peru.

---

* Coptic textiles were used by the Greek- and Egyptian-speaking Christians of Egypt between the fourth and twelfth centuries A.D. to decorate the dress of the dead. Coptic art itself (c. third to twelfth century A.D.) was a bridge between the art of the ancient world and that of the Middle Ages in western Europe.

1

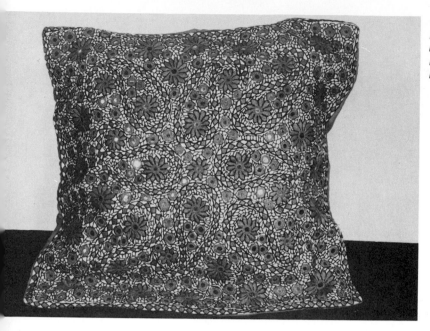

Reminiscent of Indian design, the characteristic Paisley symbol using the seedpod and also using mirrors is transmitted in this pillow from Kandahar, Afghanistan. Filled-in areas are embroidered with the long-legged cross-stitch.

Cross-stitch has been a predominant embroidery stitch used all over the world. It has, for centuries, been the surface decoration of ethnic costumes and adornments for homes from Southeast Asia to southwest Asia, the Middle East, and throughout Europe and the Americas.

In the Middle Ages, cross-stitch flourished as much in the monasteries and nunneries of Europe as in the homes (known then as *opus pulvinarium,* or cushion work). It has been practiced with love of tradition by peasants in Hungary, Romania, Bulgaria, Yugoslavia, Holland, Italy, Spain, Portugal, Scandinavia, and Russia, and was considered fit as an esteemed occupation of royalty and privileged ladies of the world. During the 15 years of her imprisonment, Mary, Queen of Scots (1542–87), created remarkable cross-stitch hangings, valances, carpets, and cushions. Besides its use for decorative patterns, cross-stitch has been a popular method of ''needle painting.'' In fact, the Romans called embroidery ''painting with needle.'' The famous Bayeux tapestry (started sometime after A.D. 1066) is really embroidery on a 20-inch-wide band on linen that is 270 feet long. On that remarkable tapestry, really a strip cartoon, a propaganda piece about feudal drama, the cooperative work of both men and women, 1,255 figures had been worked on the linen with worsted threads. In the Elizabethan period in England, canvas work appeared with cross-stitch and tent stitch (half a cross-stitch) on a linen canvas ground.

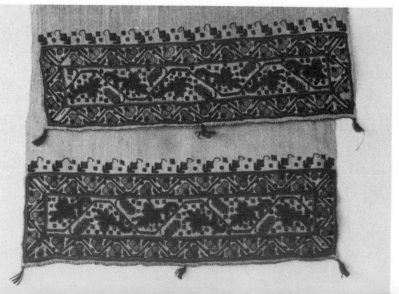

Hand-spun linen towel with silk embroidery, showing both the right and wrong side. It is nearly impossible to distinguish which side is ''up'' in the ancient traditional reversible embroidery from the Asiatic part (Anatolia) of Turkey.

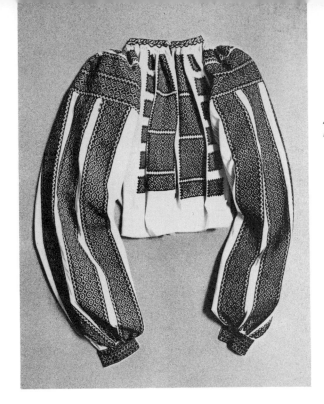

A traditional blouse from Walachia, Romania.

Cross-stitch paintings, created off and on over centuries, surfaced again as a popular art in England and America in the 1800s. These canvas-worked pieces rivaled oil portraits and sometimes copied popular paintings. Painted scenes by Sir Edwin Henry Landseer (1802–73) and his contemporaries were often rendered in cross-stitch on canvas using Berlin wool. Mrs. Theodore Roosevelt, Jr., in the 1930s, used cross-stitch as a pictorial medium, wittily representing the current scene and political issues.

Cross-stitch was as much a traditional part of a young lady's needlecraft skills in Asia as it was in Europe and America. At one time, a Chinese girl's marriageability depended upon her embroidery prowess. Indeed, many of the hill-tribe people who have migrated from China to the northern part of Thailand, Burma, and Laos still maintain that custom.

Essentially using three variations of cross-stitch, they record their memories and aspirations in symbolic patterns. More than 2,000 years of history are described using only about 50 patterns. Yet their embroidery, to this day, continues to be dynamic, alive, and vital.

An embroidered blouse by the Karens, hill-tribe people of Thailand, whose traditions date back to ancient China. Their clothing and their embellishments have changed little over the centuries.

A close-up of the Karen blouse showing wool cross-stitch outlined with fine shells on a cotton homespun fabric.

Although symbols may be copied from generation to generation by the hill tribe Yaos, as well as the T'boli people of Mindanao, Philippines, and the peasants of Europe, color and patterns are recombined into infinitely varied and complex designs. To prove her maturity, it was very important for a young lady to display skill and originality. In most places in the world, designs were usually rendered in the positive, but in Assisi, since the thirteenth and fourteenth centuries, only the background was cross-stitched in dark colors, leaving the design showing as the bare linen background.

SUBJECT MATTER AND ITS TRANSMISSION

The subject matter of cross-stitch was extremely varied. Unique designs distinguished a garment and identified the wearer, particularly as monograms and heraldic devices. They were sometimes indicators of status, occupation, or locale. Embroidered signs, such as signs of the zodiac, have for centuries been thought to protect the wearer from misfortune. Cross-stitch embroideries served beyond clothing; hangings have "warmed up" the cold stone walls of fortresses as well as the drafty walls of simple huts. They have been used as furniture covering for bed and seat and for the robes of royalty and ecclesiasts.

Styles of cross-stitch varied among geographic areas and reflected the styles and influences of the times. Yet there was a consistency among cross-stitches and their patterns. It is not unusual to see a pattern that was popular in the Middle East appear on the embroideries of Mexicans. It followed the routes of conquerors from the Moors to Spain and was brought by the Spanish to Mexico. Transmission of folk design knew no boundaries; its influences were carried by pilgrim, trader, pirate, and warrior (through pillage) from area to area.

Most folk design was schematized rather than naturalistic. It was allied to woven patterns with their dominant geometric solutions. Many of the geometric patterns were brought to Europe by pilgrims who had visited the Holy Land. Their forms were preserved as a way to revive the spirit of the past. But through travelers, the floral forms of Persia and the arabesques of southwest Asia crept into the range of design.

It was the leisure class lady who broke away from the geometric and who tried her hand at naturalistic renderings of flowers, birds, scenes, and figures, using a wider variety of rich colors that were more readily at her disposal.

Designs reflect people, locale, and their traditions, as can be seen on this silk embroidered woman's coat from Afghanistan, reflecting Persian influence.

These are the front and back views of another coat from Afghanistan. One can safely surmise that the geometric design has the longest tradition.

6

Persian floral influence can be seen in this old Turkish (reversible) embroidery.

The sampler came about when women kept a strip of linen to record motifs that came to their attention or to their minds. Samplers became a vocabulary to be passed on and often were decorative enough to be framed and hung for display. Samplers were also a way to begin and were made by children to learn the skills of cross-stitch.

Pattern books emerged during the Renaissance in the 1500s, printed as a "model book" from Venice, Paris, Cologne, and Nuremberg. This helped to further disseminate designs and also tended to conventionalize patterns and stitches. *Peterson's Magazine* in the late 1800s published patterns; one in 1867 was a needlepoint of cross-stitch pattern for a "railway traveling bag," reflecting a need for portable storage for the new traveler.

Among the pattern books, some of the most notable were designs by Hans Sibmacher of Nuremberg, published in 1591–1604. They established a standard in cross-stitch patterns and were copied continuously until the beginning of the nineteenth century. Embroideries depicting shepherds and shepherdesses, men carrying bunches of grapes, royal lions, angels, birds, trees, costumed ladies, peacocks, castles, and unicorns—became the dominant "inspiration."

For one who sought more unusual designs, an alternative was to pay for an original pattern to be designed to meet her specifications. This was a common practice in the sixteenth to eighteenth centuries. Ledger notations such as this one might have listed: "To John Hayes for drawing A Patrne for a quryssion [commission] for the quene, 7s6d."

A major change in transmission of patterns emerged when designs were represented in the nineteenth century by graphing them on squared paper, with each square representing a single stitch. This was not too different from patterns recorded for weavers. An embroiderer could, using this method, count stitches and did not have to transfer designs onto the fabric or canvas. Soon afterward, canvas was woven with a blue thread to indicate every five to ten stitches to facilitate counting and following the graphed patterns.

When printing techniques became rapid (end of nineteenth century), patterns were printed directly on fabric—usually linen or serge.

Patterns varied from age to age, with some staple designs such as the cross, the star of Bethlehem, the tree of life, the scroll, the Chinese cloud, and so on changing somewhat through interpretation but still surviving over the centuries.

Interpretations varied through the use of different dyes of certain regions and the kinds of threads available. Flax, for instance, was dominant in the lowland countries of northern Europe. When aniline dyes became popular, in the late 1800s, colors became more strident and quickly replaced the mellow vegetable-dyed colors. Silks, metal threads, wools, linen, and cotton threads each imparted a different effect. And interpretations of basic symbols using counterchange, where foil and form interplay as in a jester's suit, introduced new variations. (These were credited to Syrian-Phoenician origins.) Sometimes the background was filled in completely, and other times the unworked areas became part of the interplay of positive (design) and negative (backing) shapes, as in Assisi work.

Examples of embroidery in England and America created before the seventeenth century tended toward overall scattered patterns, influenced no doubt by the fabric prints of the period. Toward the middle of the seventeenth century, alphabets appeared more frequently, particularly as more people were learning to read. Letters and numbers often were worked into horizontal bands or borders, usually requiring counted thread work.

In the eighteenth to nineteenth centuries, colors varied from stylized use of blackwork (black on white from Spain) and white on white, using as many as five shades of white. Finer stitches were used on finely woven fabrics; bolder designs were reserved for homespun and coarser weaves.

Syrian dress, in cross-stitch, interpreted by Folkwear Patterns. Photo by Jerry Wainwright. Courtesy: Folkwear Patterns.

Silk started as a Persian monopoly, but Byzantium became the center of silk weaving after monks smuggled the silkworm from Persia to avoid high duties. Generally speaking, cotton was the most common embroidery thread, with flax and wool closely following where the preciousness and wearability of material were considerations.

The survival of cross-stitch over the centuries and its continuing popularity are due in part to the simplicity, variety, and varied potential for application of the many kinds of cross-stitches.

Embroidered pieces were used for all purposes. This silk cross-stitch Uzbek embroidery (southern Russia near Afghanistan border) is still used in wedding celebrations as decoration for horses and at other times to decorate bedrolls after they have been stacked up against the wall of the yurts (tents).

The long-legged cross-stitch is a predominant filling stitch for this symbolic elephant from India.

2 The Basic Materials for Cross-Stitch

The materials for cross-stitchery are simple yet varied. Selection depends upon several factors. What kind of object is being made? How large is it? (Large forms require a temporary covering, basted on, for protection of areas not worked.) Is the cross-stitch to be counted on canvas or on even-weave fabric? Or is it to be non-counted cross-stitch that reproduces a transferred design or one created impromptu in a "free" design?

DEFINITION

Counted thread cross-stitch (or counted cross-stitch) is precise, exact, and can be worked from charts or squared graph paper. Each basic stitch usually is represented by one square that would translate into the four holes surrounding a single warp and weft of a plain weave fabric, with each arm of the cross-stitch emanating from or terminating in these holes. This simple stitch has often been called gros point and is considered a basic stitch of the needlepoint art.

Cross-stitch, though, is not a single stitch. The vocabulary of cross-stitches includes more than 52 distinct stitches. There are ethnic preferences for some types over others, as we shall see later.

In America we often associate cross-stitch with the commonplace and simple cross-stitch—the kind we so often see with x's stamped on the fabric. We are not focusing here on that kind of stamped embroidery because it requires no explanation. Almost every aspect is preplanned and needs only the mechanical input of the embroiderer.

KINDS OF FABRICS

Even-weave or tabby-weave fabrics are constructed by the crossing of one weft (horizontal) over or under one warp (vertical) at regular intervals. The threads are the same thickness, and there are equal numbers of threads per inch for warp as for weft. It is called a *square count*. Embroidery on this type of fabric can easily be used for a symmetrical, geometric shape.

A variety of plain-weave linen fabrics (from Joan Toggitt Ltd.). Left to right, two natural color linens, Artikel 3613 "Cork" fine white linen (3609/51), and a fine cream-colored linen (3609/52).

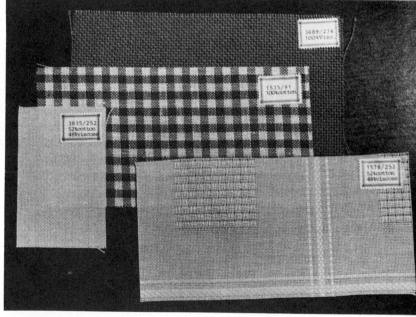

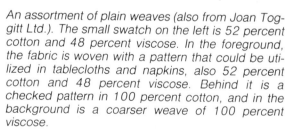

An assortment of plain weaves (also from Joan Toggitt Ltd.). The small swatch on the left is 52 percent cotton and 48 percent viscose. In the foreground, the fabric is woven with a pattern that could be utilized in tablecloths and napkins, also 52 percent cotton and 48 percent viscose. Behind it is a checked pattern in 100 percent cotton, and in the background is a coarser weave of 100 percent viscose.

There are two basic classes of materials used for embroidery—natural fibers and synthetics, resulting in a wide variety of choices. Traditionally, cross-stitch was worked on linen, wool, cotton, and silk. Of late, the various synthetics have expanded the potential range into an embarrassment of riches.

Some examples of even-weave fabrics are *monk's cloth*, which has a 2 × 2 square count and is woven in various weights. *Hardanger cloth* is another type with warp and weft threads woven in a square count. *Aida cloth* is also a basket-weave fabric constructed with interlocking threads woven in such a way that holes appear almost as clearly as in canvas. Hardanger, monk's, and Aida cloth are woven with flat threads.

Linen, although a square count as well, has rounder threads and the thickness of each thread of the warp or weft may vary somewhat.

Two popular plain weaves—on the left 100 percent cotton Aida cloth and on the right 100 percent cotton fine Hardanger weave.

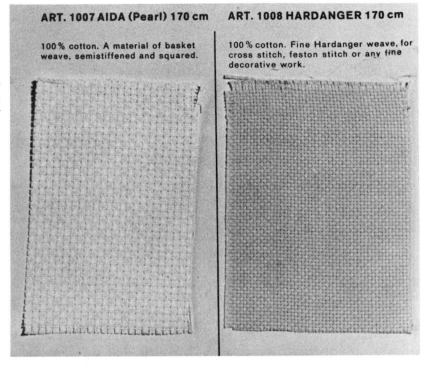

ART. 1007 AIDA (Pearl) 170 cm — 100% cotton. A material of basket weave, semistiffened and squared.

ART. 1008 HARDANGER 170 cm — 100% cotton. Fine Hardanger weave, for cross stitch, feston stitch or any fine decorative work.

Fabrics appropriate for cross-stitch differ in fineness from ten to more than 42 threads per inch. They also come in various widths from 52-inch for Belgian linen to 36-inch for some synthetics.

When fabric is too finely woven to permit counting for cross-stitch, an auxiliary waste canvas can be basted to the fabric and then its warp and weft threads pulled away when the embroidery has been completed.

Most fabrics can be purchased by the yard. There is no need to buy more than what one requires.

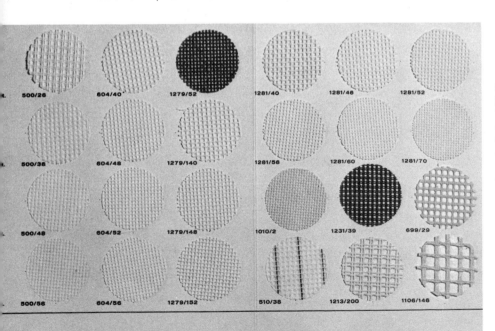

500/26   604/40   1279/52   1281/40   1281/46   1281/52
500/36   604/48   1279/140   1281/56   1281/60   1281/70
500/48   604/52   1279/148   1010/2   1231/39   699/29
500/56   604/56   1279/152   510/38   1213/200   1106/146

100% PURE COTTON CANVAS

A sample card showing a range of 100 percent cotton canvas from Penelope with 7 stitches per inch (top left), to mono interlock with 10 stitches per inch (2nd top row left), to bargello tan mono canvas, 14 stitches per inch (3rd from left top row) to rug canvas (lower right), 4 stitches per inch, to blue striped waste canvas with 10 stitches to inch (bottom row, 4th sample from left), to brown double mesh with 10 stitches per inch (second row from right, second sample from right). From Joan Toggitt Ltd.

Petit point canvas usually comes in 24-inch width with 17 to 22 stitches per inch. Available recently is a very fine silk gauze used for miniature petit point making or other very fine work, containing 34, 40, and 44 stitches per inch respectively, in 40-inch widths. From Joan Toggitt Ltd.

Canvas used for needlepoint, is woven in single-or double-weave squares of linen, cotton, silk, or hemp, and has open holes called *mesh*. Canvases are available in a variety of thicknesses and threads per inch. *Penelope* is the name for double-weave canvas and *mono* for single-weave canvas. Some variations are used for bulky yarn. These are made of plastic, perforated paper, or hemp. The mesh size indicates the number of holes per inch. Ten-mesh, for example, is finer than 4-mesh because it contains ten holes per inch instead of four.

Some canvas is white, others yellow, cream, or tan colored. Some have blue guidelines woven through, forming a grid to help demarcate units and thereby facilitate the counting process. Other canvases are called waste canvas because cross-stitch can be worked through the canvas to the fabric beneath it, using the canvas only as a vehicle to make counting easier. After the embroidery is finished, the warp and weft of the canvas are pulled out from beneath the stitches revealing an embroidered cloth.

KINDS OF YARNS AND THREADS

Yarn implies that the original fibers or filaments have been more or less loosely twisted together. *Thread* is more tightly twisted fibers or filaments, resulting in a finer, smoother strand. Each strand of yarn or thread is called a *ply*. They often come in two-, three-, four- or eight-ply. Usually, one can separate or untwist the strands or plies in order to control the thickness.

A small assortment of rayon threads in various textures, fineness, and a wide range of beautiful colors.

The range of yarns and threads is tremendous, as can be seen from this list:

natural linen
embroidery cotton (mercerized floss)
Pearl cotton
cotton chenille
crochet cotton
cotton warp
butcher's twine (cotton)
linen (smoother)—Knox is one brand from Scotland
linen warp
rayon bouclé
rayon—high sheen to low sheen, almost matte
rayon chenille
acetate
raw silk
"refined" silk—high sheen to low sheen
acrylic rug yarn
acrylic knitting/crochet yarn
polyester rug yarn
polyester knitting/crochet yarn
worsted (wool and wool mixtures) in many different ply and thicknesses
mohair
novelty fibers such as tinsel threads (in various metallic colors), raffia,
    jute, nylon (as fishing line)

Various yarns and threads are processed for specific purposes, such as worsted for tapestry, gros point, and petit point, wool for crewel, and so on. That does not mean uses are not interchangeable—they are, if the texture is suitable.

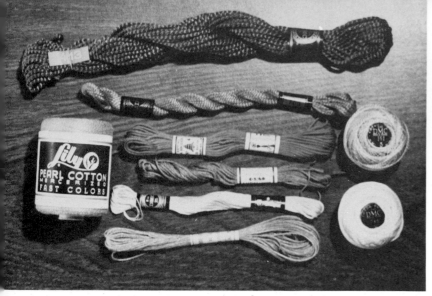

An assortment of cotton threads, showing a range of texture and fineness.

Some brands of wool fibers are softer, stronger, have longer fibers (won't frizz), and some have a wider range of colors running to hundreds of subtle variations in hue, value, and intensity, e.g., DMC and Belding. Some are colorfast; others will bleed in water. Most are aniline dyed; very few are natural dyed.

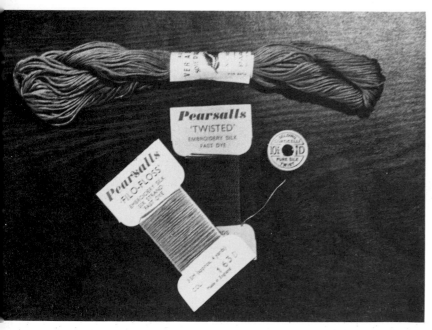

Some silk threads, including Belding Lily's buttonhole twist, which comes on a small wooden spool.

Thickness of thread or yarn corresponds to coarseness or fineness of the fabric or canvas. Numbers 14-mesh to 18-mesh canvases are suitable for handbags, pillows, eyeglass cases, book covers, articles of clothing; one-, two-, or three-ply wool, such as Persian wool, is suitable. (In Persian yarn each strand is two-ply.) Numbers 10 and 8 canvas are more appropriate for rugs, larger pillows, shopping bags, and wall hangings where fine detail is not built into the design. In any case, the thread or yarn should cover the canvas so that the canvas does not show through, but it should not be so thick that one thread obliterates the other. Some stitches also have different requisites for thickness of thread or yarn, depending on the size and detail of the stitch. No easy formula can be given; each design requires its own decisions. One rule of thumb is that roughly one-half pound of yarn will cover one square foot of canvas—

depending upon the stitch. In any case, it is advisable to purchase all one requires of a color at one time because dye lots change subtly from time to time and colors sometimes oxidize with age.

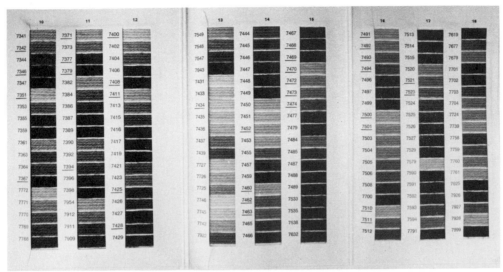

Just a few of hundreds of wool yarns in a range of hues, values, and chroma from DMC. The wide range of colors makes for the possibility for shading in fine graduations resulting in subtle blending of colors.

The length of thread one uses to thread a needle is also a personal preference, but there are some considerations. Threads and yarns that fuzz, fray, or tangle should be worked in shorter lengths. Otherwise, I prefer long lengths because they result in a neater appearance on the back and impart a sense of continuity that is achieved when one does not have to begin and end repeatedly.

A way to keep color selections untangled and ready for use. This is a piece of acrylic drilled with ½-inch holes. One can also use well-sanded wood or even heavy cardboard. A different color of thread is looped through each hole.

NEEDLES

There is one essential needle for counted cross-stitch, whether on canvas or tabby-weave fabrics—this is the tapestry needle. It has a long eye and a blunt point and comes in sizes numbered 13 to 24 (the lower the number, the bigger the needle). The reason for a blunt point is that the fabric is *not* to be pierced. The needle should guide the thread or yarn through the holes.

For those design problems that transcend fabric and are followed by a transfer pattern of some kind, use crewel needles that are long-eyed and have pointed ends (number 3 to number 9), or chenille needles that are large-eyed and sharply pointed (number 18 to number 22) but shorter than crewel needles. (Sharps, the needle type used for sewing, small eye and sharp point, are sometimes used for fine threads.)

The test of an appropriate-sized needle is whether the thread or yarn will pass through the eye without fraying or snagging. Size 18 is best for 10-mesh canvas and is a good general-purpose needle; sizes 19, 20, 22 are best for 12-, 14-, 16-, and 18-mesh canvas respectively; sizes 13, 14, and 15 are good for rug yarn used on 7-, 5-, and 3-mesh (quick point) rug canvases.

ACCESSORIES

Frames and Hoops

Use of a frame or embroidery hoop is a matter of preference. I usually prefer to work without one because an unstretched fabric or canvas allows for two thrusts of the needle at each stroke, whereas a tautly framed piece necessitates penetrating the fabric from top or bottom, drawing the thread through, and then reversing the direction—each a different operation that I find cumbersome. Without a frame I can much more easily "feel" the stitch—its tension and position—but, admittedly, this technique requires practice to achieve uniform tension of stitches. It may be easier to maintain a consistent tension with a hoop or frame. With the hoop, one aspect is controlled when the background fabric is pulled taut and even so that warp and weft form right angles to one another. If you use a hoop, use a small one; it has the advantage of being more flexible and more portable—it can be transported anywhere.

Transfer Materials and Accessories

Pencil, coloring tools such as paint, dye-papers, crayons, or colored markers for

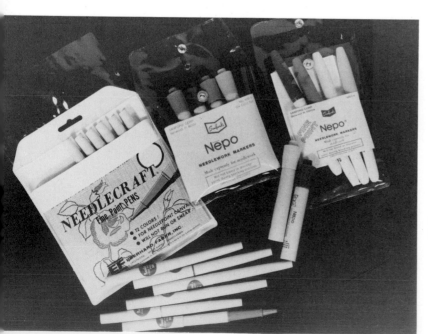

Needlecraft and Nēpo markers for drawing or transferring designs onto fabric or canvas.

fabric (more about these later in chapter 4), graph paper, rulers, tape measures, and perhaps an iron for pressing fabric or dye may be required, depending on specific needs.

Other

Scissors (small for snipping threads and yarns and large for trimming backgrounds), thimble to guard against a callused finger, masking tape to bind cut edges of canvas or fabric, magnifying glass to aid in needle threading, and needle-threading devices to facilitate the threading of the eye complete the limited list of ''tools.''

3
Stitches

Stitches are the *raison d'être* of embroidery—the ways of using threads and yarns decoratively. Stitches often carry the name of their place of origin, e.g., the Montenegrine cross-stitch. Others may have several names. The rice stitch is also known as crossed-corners stitch or the William and Mary stitch. Names given to stitches don't always correspond from place to place. The cross-stitch is called *al pasado* in Spanish, *gros point* when used on canvas, *saddle stitch* on leather, and sometimes *sampler stitch* when used on a sampler.

Stitches are essentially short or long, slanted, horizontal, and vertical. Combinations result in broad classifications which as *flat stitches*. These lay flat on the surface of the material. Most cross-stitches fall into this category.

There are also *looped* stitches. These are flat but loop together such as the buttonhole or feather stitch. *Chained* or *linked stitches* are those that link with loops, such as the leaf stitch. *Knotted stitches* are raised and contain a decorative knot as an essential element; an example is the French knot. *Detached* stitches are woven or looped into a foundation of stitches such as the Maltese cross, and *composite* is, as the classification suggests, combinations of the first four groups.

Some stitches contain only two strokes; others require multiple strokes which are still considered a single stitch, such as the Smyrna stitch. Short, slanted stitches require a finer thread than long, straight stitches. Each stitch has a distinct contour that can be varied through the choice of thread or yarn, color, scale, and how compactly or loosely constructed the stitches are.

Some stitches arc more appropriate for certain applications. The fern cross-stitch, for example, lends itself to leafy rendering, whereas the long-armed (long-legged) cross-stitch is particularly adaptable as a filler stitch where small to large spaces need to be covered.

The assortment of stitches that follows may not contain every cross-stitch ever invented. It does, however, present a pretty thorough array—52 variations of cross-stitches. They are presented here in a unique way, as a breakdown of the stitch for almost every stroke required. All you need to know in order to follow the sequence of each stitch is that (1) the dot represents the needle coming *up* from *behind* the fabric and (2) the arrow indicates where the needle *penetrates* the fabric from the *top* surface. (3) Sometimes dotted lines are indicated. These detail where the thread journeys underneath (on the back). (4) Dashes represent the stitch in progress. If you follow the stitch starting from dot and ending with the arrow for each stroke, you'll discover that even the most complicated multiple stitches are easy. Specific hints are given where necessary.

Basic Diagonal Cross-stitch (originally referred to as Gros Point or Petit Point)

The basic diagonal cross-stitch consists of two slanting stitches, one over the other, crossing in the center.

This stitch can be worked in two ways: half the cross completed across the row and then the other half completed on the return journey; or each cross as a unit can be completed before moving on to the next one.

There are many variations, even for this simple stitch. In these two stitches, all strokes cross in the same direction, in the cross-stitch-gone-wrong, the strokes can alternate, left to right, diagonal may be under or over the right to left cross. This results in different pattern-texture effects.

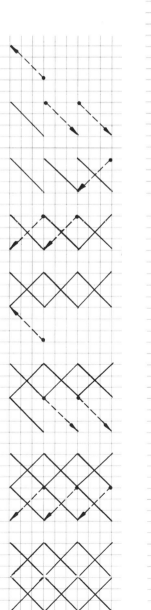
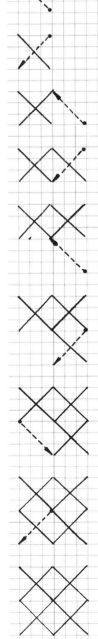

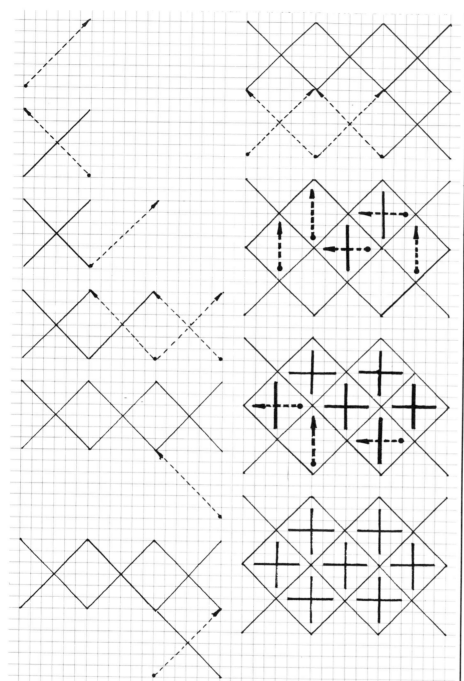

Large Cross-stitch with Straight Cross-stitch

Yet another combination can be achieved by combining a large diagonal cross-stitch with a smaller straight (or even diagonal) cross-stitch and varying color, texture, and kinds of thread. One can also reverse the order and use a large vertical cross-stitch to demarcate areas that are filled in with small diagonal cross-stitches.

Basic Diagonal Cross-stitches with Ba (Italian Cross-stitch)

Three variations using the diagonal cross, which surrounded by vertical and horizontal bars, can treated in several ways. On the left, stitches sha common bands in the overall pattern, and in center, each unit is worked separately, surround by its own set of bars. Or, on the right, the stitch are treated as a border, turning a corner.

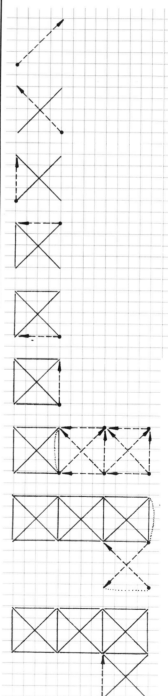

Variation 2

Variation 3

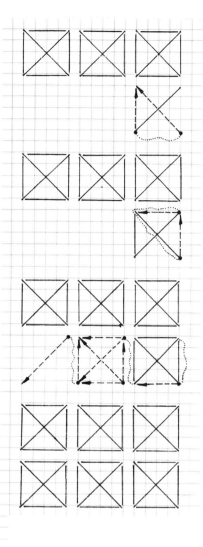

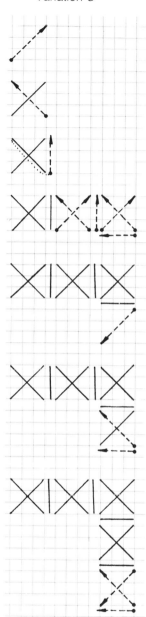

Reversed Cross-stitch (Double Cross-stitch)

In this case, the background larger cross-stitch is straight and a smaller diagonal cross-stitch is superimposed with all intersections overlapping and meeting at the crossing point. Another variation is to start with a larger straight cross-stitch and superimpose a smaller diagonal cross-stitch. This makes for an excellent canvas or filling stitch.

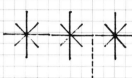

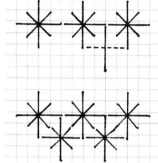

Smyrna Cross-stitch (Double Cross-stitch)

The Smyrna cross-stitch is similar to the reversed cross-stitch except that each stitch is the same size whereas in the reversed cross-stitch there is a contrast in size between the two superimposed cross-stitches. This stitch is sometimes mistakingly known as Leviathan.

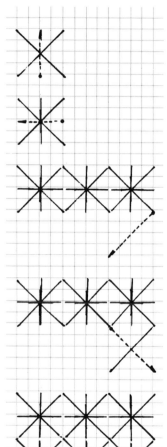

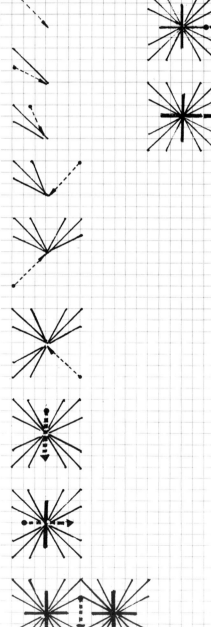

Leviathan (Algerian Eye with Straight Cross-stitch)

In the Leviathan, diagonal stitches meet at a common point and the juncture is covered with a straight cross-stitch. The space between stitches is also filled with a straight cross. This makes for a good canvas or filling stitch.

Knotted

One diagonal of the knotted stitch is at least two and a half to three times longer than the crossing diagonal, thereby creating a slanted effect. The proportions can vary somewhat so long as one diagonal stroke is decidedly longer than the other. This can be used as a canvas or filling stitch.

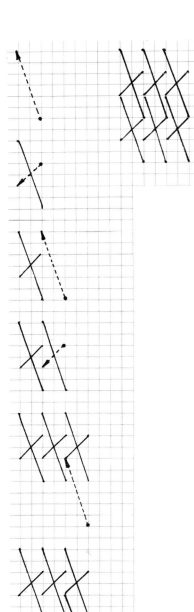

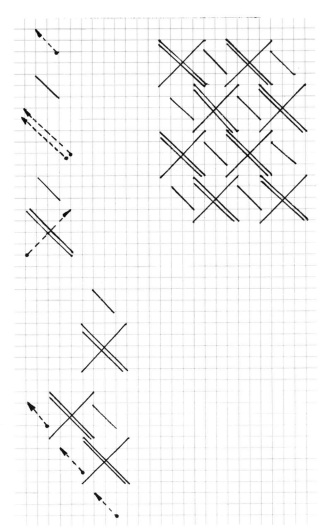

Hobnail

A small diagonal cross-stitch with two diagonals under another single diagonal makes for a hobnail or bumpy effect. Another small diagonal (tent stitch) between each hobnail fills in the open areas.

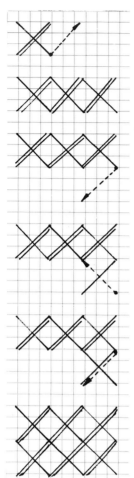

Hobnail Variation (Reinforced Cross-stitch)

The direction of the double understitches is reversed, and each stitch shares common holes with the previous stitch. The same is true on the return journey.

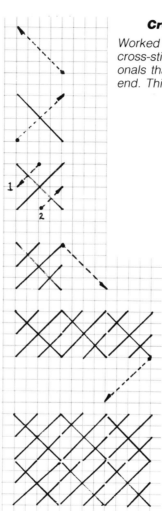

Cross Scotch Stitch (Crossed Mosaic)

Worked in horizontal rows, one stroke of a diagonal cross-stitch is crossed at both ends with smaller diagonals that result in smaller diagonal crosses at each end. This is a good canvas or filling stitch.

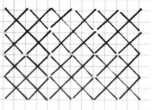

Rice Stitch (Crossed Corners Stitch, William and Mary Stitch)

This is similar to the crossed Scotch stitch except that small diagonals are crossed over both longer diagonal strokes (rather than over one as in the crossed Scotch stitch).

This stitch is often worked with a heavier thread for the larger diagonals and a finer thread for the small crossing diagonals. This is a good canvas or filling stitch.

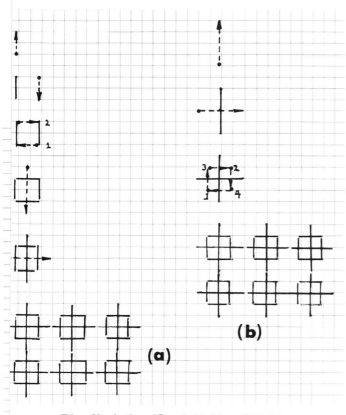

(b)

(a)

Rice Variation (Straight Rice Stitch)

This is a variation of the rice stitch using straight crosses instead of diagonal crosses.

The difference between (a) and (b) is just which stitches are applied first—the crossing strokes as in (a) or the larger straight cross as in (b). The effect would be different in each, particularly if different thicknesses or colors of thread were used.

Bucky's Weaving

The effect is an overall pattern that appears to be woven. The vertical and horizontal bars that thread in and out of the fabric or canvas can be two, three, or four rows wide, depending on the effect desired. A diagonal cross fills in the spaces demarcated by the woven bands.

A variation can be achieved by using straight cross-stitches instead of diagonals.

(The numbers indicate the sequence of each journey, which consists of two strokes each.) This pattern can be expanded to larger units by just continuing each journey to include more strokes.

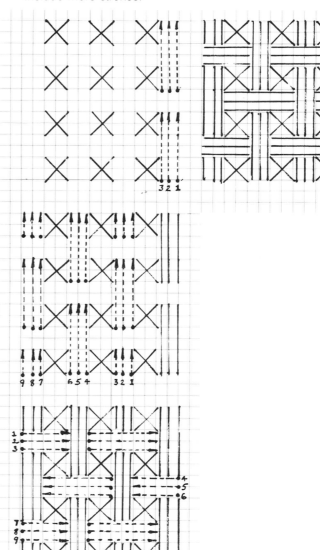

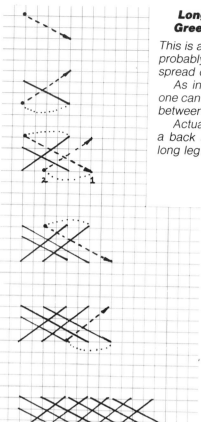

Long-armed Cross-stitch (Long-legged Cross-stitch, Greek Cross-stitch, Plaited Slav Stitch, Twist Stitch)

This is a popular stitch, known by several names. Its popularity is probably due to the fact that it is so versatile because it can be spread out or compressed and acts as an excellent filling stitch.

As in the Montenegrin, in order to square off the beginning, one can start with compensating stitches. The essential difference between the two stitches is that there is no horizontal bar.

Actually, this is a cross-stitch that, after each insertion, requires a back stitching to the last stitch, thereby overlapping the one long leg. Once you get the rhythm, it is very simple to do.

Ermine Stitch

This stitch is basically a cross-stitch superimposed at the lower end of a bar or satin stitch.

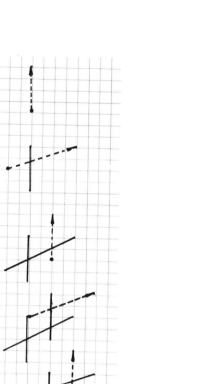

Diagonal Long-legged Cross-stitch

Besides adapting well to filling in areas, the long-legged cross-stitch can also be worked diagonally and can be repeated to create zigzag effects.

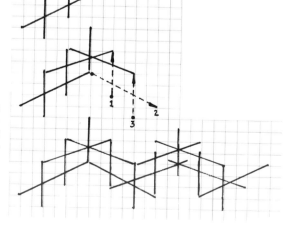

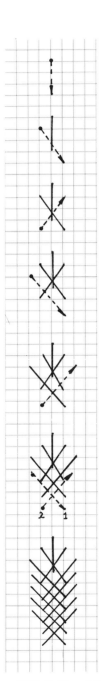

This stitch speaks for itself. It is actually a series of diagonal cross-stitches used to couch or hold in place an underlying thread. The arms of the cross-stitch can be varied in size, and the juncture of crossing can change as can the direction of the underlying thread.

Double Fishbone

The single fishbone is not strictly a cross-stitch (as can be seen in the first few diagrams), but when a second layer (thread change or color change) is added, the strokes do, in fact, cross, much as in the fern stitch or as you will see in the herringbone.

It is a good stitch for filling in small shapes and can make for a decorative repeat pattern over broader areas.

Diagonal Fishbone

Although unlike the double fishbone, where the strokes are diagonal, these strokes are vertical and horizontal but are worked in a diagonal direction.

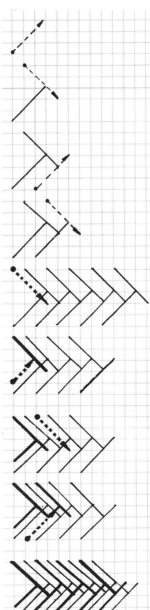

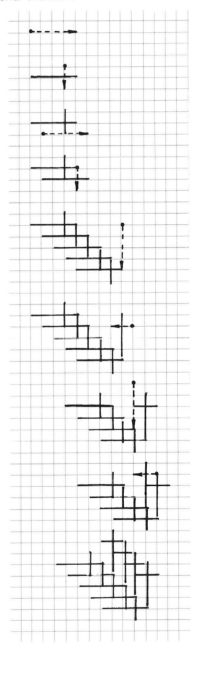

Fern Stitch (Leaf Stitch)

Similar to the ermine stitch, the leaf stitch begins with a shorter bar and the crosses continue to overlay one another.

Variations can be achieved by eliminating the beginning bar, by changing the point of crossing, and by changing the direction of the unit, such as from vertical to diagonal.

Herringbone

This stitch is usually worked over larger areas so that the herringbone effect can become evident.

It is sometimes used for shadow work on transparent fabric where the back becomes the front and the structure of the stitches is seen through the transparent fabric. It is also a good canvas or filling stitch.

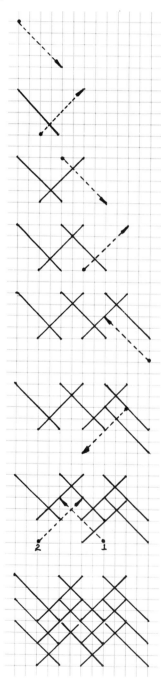

Double Herringbone

In the double herringbone stitch, two contrasting textures or colors are used. The spacing can also be varied so that threads (strokes) are closer or farther apart.

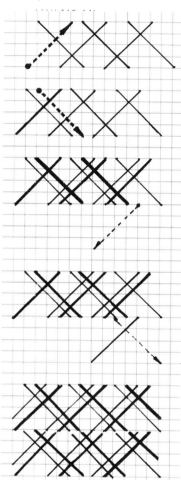

Squared Herringbone

A single unit is described here. Units, however, can be repeated on canvas by filling in spaces between units with bars and crosses.

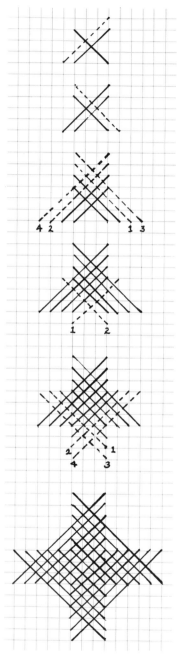

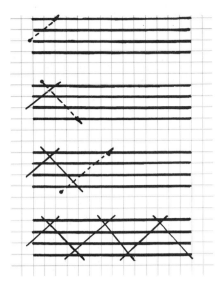

Herringbone Couching

Another variation on the herringbone theme is to use the herringbone stitch as couching over a horizontal group of threads, as shown here, or even over a vertical group of threads.

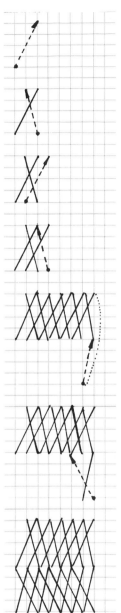

Basket Stitch

This is like an opened-up herringbone or even a plait stitch that is opened up. These are all of the same family with slight variations on the basic concept.

Plait Stitch (Plaited Slav Stitch, Algerian Plait)

This is similar to the Montenegrin and the long-legged cross, except that only the top or bottom of the diagonal cross overlapped and there is no bar as in the Montenegrin.

In the return journey, variations can be achieved by varying the direction of the stroke and which stroke is on top.

The Algerian plait is like a tall herringbone that is closed up.

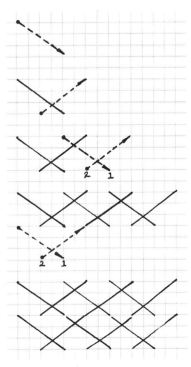

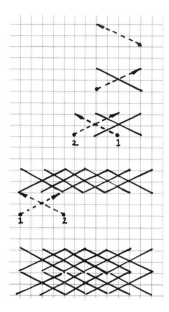

Knitting Stitch

Also part of the same family, the knitting stitch is worked in horizontal rows with every other cross sharing the same hole rather than crossing the previous stitch. The overall effect looks like knitting.

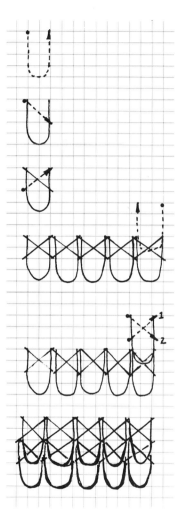

Astrakhan Velvet (Velvet Stitch)

This is but one approach to creating a looped stitch that is held in place by a diagonal cross-stitch at the top. In the return journey, the loops overlap, often covering the cross-stitches. This is the only three-dimensional cross-stitch.

In order to maintain an even length to the loop, a pencil can be used as a gauge to wrap the thread around (and be removed later). I judge size using my eye and hold the loop in place with my thumb until the top of the stitch is reinforced.

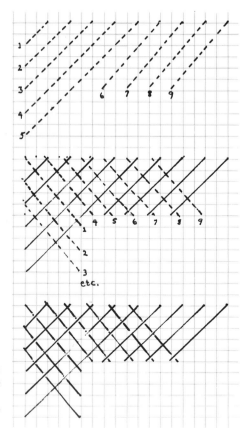

Woven Band (Web Stitch)

This is usually a canvas-work stitch that produces a woven effect. The foundation stitches grow larger and smaller to adapt to the space being filled.

Variations can be achieved by alternating colors or textures of threads.

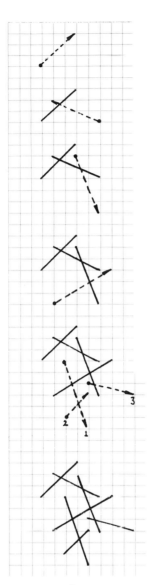

Random Cross-stitch

Here diagonals of various lengths and directions cross at random points. It provides a free, textured way of filling in background, particularly for contemporary effects.

Invent a Cross-stitch: Thelma Newman's Looped Cross-stitch

Each stroke of this new diagonal cross-stitch is actually a loop that is linked at the center (crossing point) by each of the four strokes. Each of the four loops starts and ends in the same hole. In the end, even tension on each of the loops maintains the cross effect as the loops link to one another. This looped-cross imparts a lacy quality.

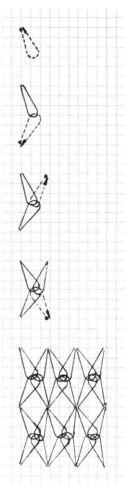

Sampler of Stitches

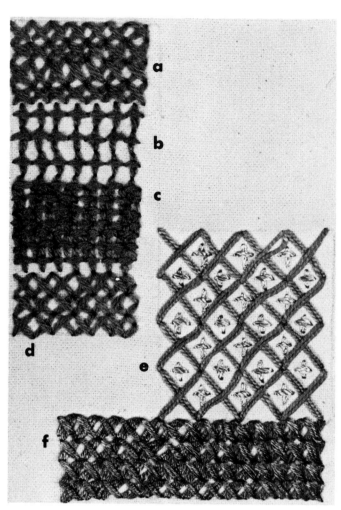

a. Diagonal cross-stitch in Carol Rome Enterprises 2-ply 3-strand wool.
b. Straight cross-stitch in the same thread as above.
c. Straight cross-stitch variation in the same thread as above.
d. Cross-stitch gone wrong in the same thread as above.
e. Large cross-stitch with straight cross-stitch variation. The large cross-stitch is worked in Lily Pearl Cotton and the small cross-stitch in Springer Bella-Donna rayon.
f. Reinforced cross-stitch in Springer Ostara.

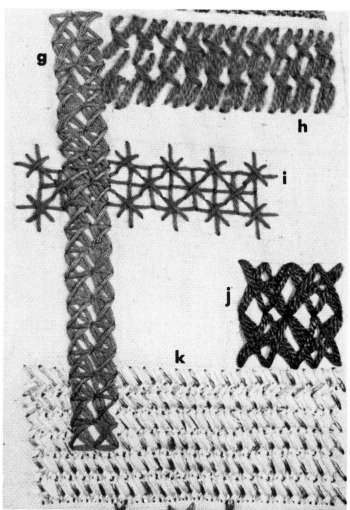

g. Montenegrin variation in Ver a Soie by Soie d'Alger.
h. Knotted cross-stitch in DMC Floralia.
i. Double straight cross-stitch in Retours a Broder cotton.
j. Triple cross-stitch in DMC Coton Perle.
k. Double fishbone in two colors, one in Lily Pearl Cotton and the other in rayon.

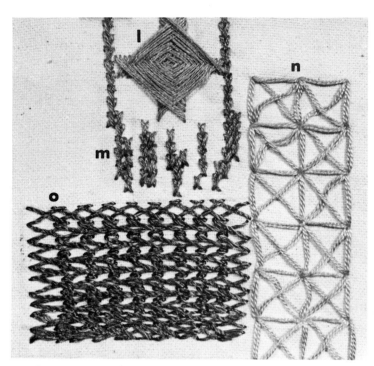

l. Squared herringbone in Swedish linen.
m. Knitting stitch in an overlapped and condensed treatment
   using Swedish linen.
n. Italian cross-stitch in DMC Coton Perle.
o. Knitting stitch in rayon.

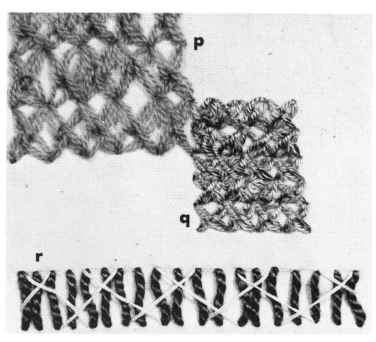

p. Thelma Newman's looped cross-stitch in 2-ply wool.
q. Thelma Newman's looped cross-stitch in Springer Ostara.
r. Straight stitch couched with long-legged cross-stitch using
   different colors and thicknesses of cotton thread.

Summary of Stitches and Particular Applications

C—canvas   F—filling of areas   P—plain-weave fabrics

Basic Diagonal Cross-stitch   C-F-P
Reversible Diagonal Cross-stitch (Two-sided)   P
Diagonally Placed Diagonal Cross-stitch   P
Staggered Diagonal Cross-stitch   P
Basic Straight Cross-stitch   C-F-P
Straight Cross-stitch Variation   C-F-P
Diagonal Straight Cross-stitch   P
Straight Cross Variation   C-F-P
St. George and St. Andrew   C-F-P
Large Cross-stitch with Straight Cross-stitch   C-F-P
Basic Diagonal Cross-stitches with Bars   P
Straight Cross with Bars in Diagonal Setting   C-F-P
Zigzag   P
Oblong Diagonal Cross-stitch   C-F-P
Oblong Diagonal Cross-stitch with Basic Diagonal Cross-stitch   C-F-P
Oblong Diagonal Cross-stitch Variation with Bars   C-F-P
Oblong Diagonal Cross-stitch with Single Back Stitch   C-F-P
Oblong Diagonal Cross-stitch with Double Back Stitch   C-F-P
Larger Diagonal Cross-stitch with Straight Cross Variations   C-F-P
Reversed Cross-stitch   C-F-P
Smyrna Cross-stitch   C-F-P
Leviathan   C-F-P
Knotted   C-F-P
Hobnail   C-F-P
Hobnail Variation   C-F-P
Crossed Scotch Stitch   C-F-P
Rice Stitch   C-F-P
Rice Variation   C-F-P
Bucky's Weaving   C-F-P
Sheaf Stitch   P
One-sided Insertion Stitch   P or C-F-P as repeat
Triple Cross-stitch   C-F-P
Montenegrin   P or C-F-P as repeat
Montenegrin Variation   P or C-F-P as repeat
Long-armed Cross-stitch   P
Diagonal Long-legged Cross-stitch   P
Ermine Stitch   P
Thorn Stitch   P
Fern Stitch   C-F-P
Double Fishbone   C-F-P
Diagonal Fishbone   C-F-P
Herringbone   C-F-P
Double Herringbone   C-F-P
Squared Herringbone   P or with repeat or with compensating stitches   C-F-P
Herringbone Couching   P
Plait Stitch   C-F-P
Basket Stitch   P
Knitting Stitch   C-F-P
Woven Band   C-F-P
Astrakhan Velvet   C-F-P
Random Cross-stitch   P
Thelma Newman's Looped Cross-stitch   P

4
Beginnings: Designs and Translations

This probably is the most interesting aspect of needlework—planning and designing what is to be made. After translation of the design to the background or the plotting of the design, the rest is mechanical execution (which can also be fun) and the test of your needlework prowess. What inspires us to come up with the nucleus of an idea and begin a particular needlework might vary from time to time. It may be that a particular stitch or combination could stimulate an idea. A particular object could suggest a solution by dint of its shape. Or it could be that a cluster of weeds or a flower would inspire a design.

PLANNING

Suitable Objects

At any rate, what we are to be making is a significant decision, whether the piece is to be an eyeglass case, upholstery fabric, or decorative detail on clothing. Here are some items that lend themselves to cross-stitch embroidery:

> Clothing—borders, pocket, insignia, overall design, apron
> Book covers—album, address book, special book jacket such as for a Bible
> Umbrella cover

Coasters, hot plate, tray—covered with glass or clear acrylic
Tennis/badminton covers
Game boards—backgammon, checkers, chess, etc., covered with acrylic
Pillows
Handbags, tote bags
Upholstery
Linens—trim on sheets, pillowcases, towels
Hangings and pictures
Memory plaques—to commemorate special occasions
Signs—such as ''No smoking'' or ''Welcome''
Nameplates
Wallets
Belts
Tablecloths and napkins
Aprons
Cabinet doors, screens
Curtains
Behind clear plastic of light switches and door plates
And others

Appropriate Designs

Needleworkers who are continually productive keep an idea file and store ''in-reserve'' designs for their future work. Sources for designs are virtually everywhere. They may come from illustrations in books and magazines; be stimulated by posters, paintings, and drawings; be found on old fabrics, china, and silver; be culled from photographs, greeting cards, gift wrap paper, flowers and vegetable seed catalogs; be fashioned from folk art, architectural detail; and be inspired by the two greatest resources of all—nature and your own imagination.

From this plethora of ideas, the most appropriate design is sketched (or clipped out) to suit the object and its shape. Generally, bold designs are more suitable for larger forms such as rugs, and more finely detailed designs fit objects that would be seen from close up. In any case, there should be an impact—the right feeling about purpose, shape, pattern, texture, and color.

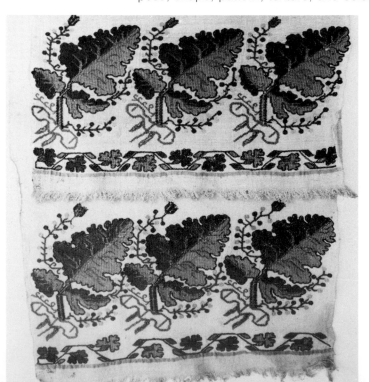

This old Turkish embroidery seen on both the front and undersides, stylizes a leaf design, contrasts colors in a counterchange effect, and repeats the design. Smaller floral shapes fill in spaces and help to unite the separate elements.

Ways to Design

Start with a shape. It could be a geometric shape. Think about patterns created by the shape and how the shapes relate to one another and the background. Enlarge it, combine it with smaller versions, overlap it, repeat it in various ways. Select from your manipulations the most appealing design and assign colors to the parts. Think also in terms of texture (particularly when you select stitches).

This lady's jacket from Afghanistan utilizes silk floral elements on cotton in a formally balanced repeat format. The round flower shapes actually frame the interior elements of leaves that are arranged almost in a repeat pattern.

Another way to begin is by cutting a shape from paper—snip out details—cut the design into parts and rearrange them along with the snipped away details. One part can become the positive with its details cut out and then arranged in counterchanged form, as a flipped, or mirror, image.

Another approach is to divide the space to be embroidered by repeating a theme, perhaps by arranging it into stripes, zigzags, checkerboard, or other more random repeat effects.

Another cross-stitch jacket from Afghanistan divides the area into four broad divisions and almost in checkerboard fashion repeats the same symbol in contrasting colors.

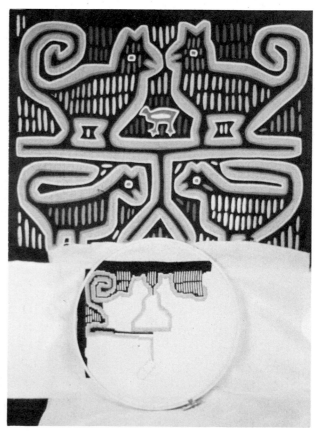

A mola in reverse appliqué from San Blas in Panama inspired a gros point design. The design was not followed slavishly but served as a starting point. Note how the size reduced down to a quarter of the original piece.

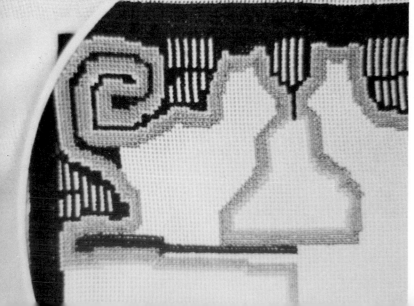

A close-up showing canvas and the cross-stitch. The final example by Lee Newman can be seen in chapter 8.

Look at nature in macrocosm or microcosm. Plowed fields may suggest translation to a contour pattern that would be attractive for a seat cover; or a microscopic particle such as a cell or a snowflake might inspire an adaptation.

Also, slice an apple and pear and note the seedpod effect in cross section. Or design an X-ray effect, such as a pea pod describing the pea shapes in the unopened pod.

This acrylic tetrahedron inspired the geometric cross-stitch on canvas design by Jay Newman.

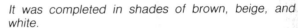

It was completed in shades of brown, beige, and white.

Note dried weed pods. Arrange them into clusters; abstract the most essential elements. How would these shapes look best—as borders, fillings, and allover patterns, or as discrete units?

One can go on and on. There is really no limit to fresh and vital design potential, whether it would be inspired by something commonplace or exotic.

Proportion of a design changes, in effect, as shown in these three versions of the same cotton cross-stitch border on white linen.

Color

Choice of color can make or break a potentially strong design concept. On the other hand, almost any color combination will look good for the appropriate design purpose.

Some surefire solutions are to start with a single color. Variations can be achieved by using tints and tones of the same color but by allowing one particular value to predominate. Another successful decision is to try related color schemes, analogous (contiguous) colors on the color wheel such as violet, blue violet, blue. Or for more dynamic effects, select a color and introduce its complement (opposite on the color wheel—blue and orange, red and green, yellow and violet). This creates a vibrant effect. Try using contrasting effects such as black and white, yellow and dark brown, and so on. Look carefully at nature or at artists' paintings and try to distill the amount and kind of colors you see.

Often using related (analogous) colors of the same value, side by side, one can achieve a vibrant impact.

Texture

Texture is what you are adding to the background. It's an intrinsic aspect of attaching thread or yarn to a ground. How well you capitalize on the potential for texture are the choices you make in combining threads and yarns and/or the selection of stitches. Even with the seeming restriction of one class of stitches, cross-stitch, you can achieve furry, smooth, rough, corrugated, honeycombed effects. As you look through the illustrations that follow, note the particular stitches that impart a sense of texture.

Developing Design Ideas
Abstracting Shapes into Geometric Effects

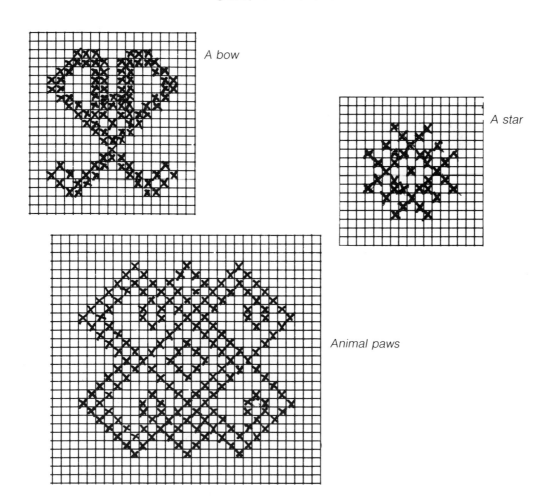

A bow

A star

Animal paws

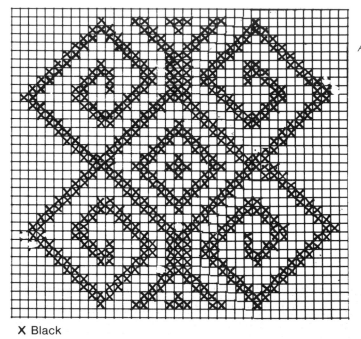

A butterfly

X Black

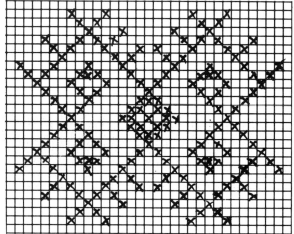

Another variation of a butterfly

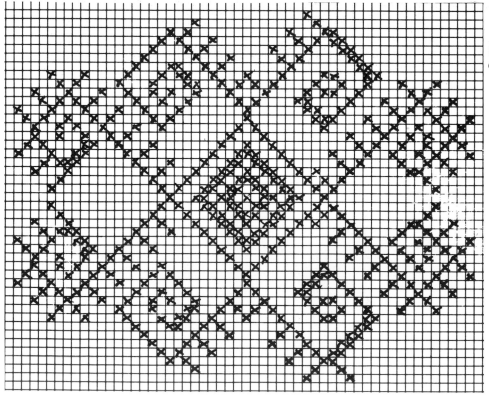

Combining elements of all these designs.

Variations on a Theme; Using the Greek Key

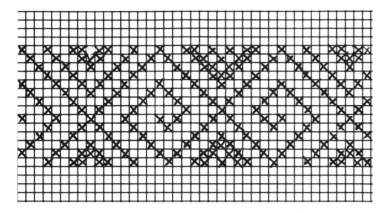

The Greek key is central. Triangles fill in areas around the simple key.

The Greek key is still rendered in simple form, but the space between the Greek keys becomes more dominant with repeated zigzags.

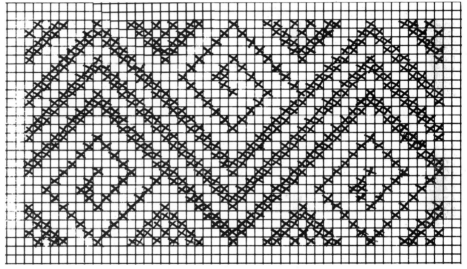

Here the key is doubled in thickness and is embellished with projections. The zigzag becomes a repeat design for what could become an effective border design.

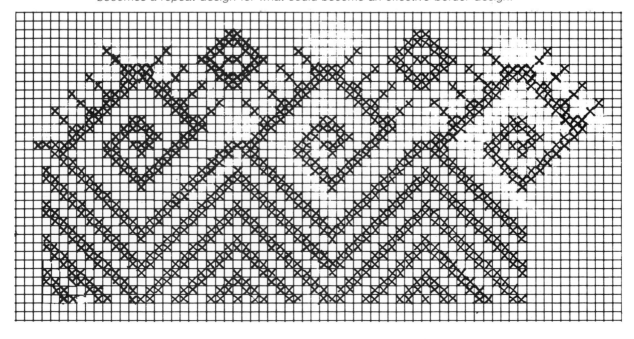

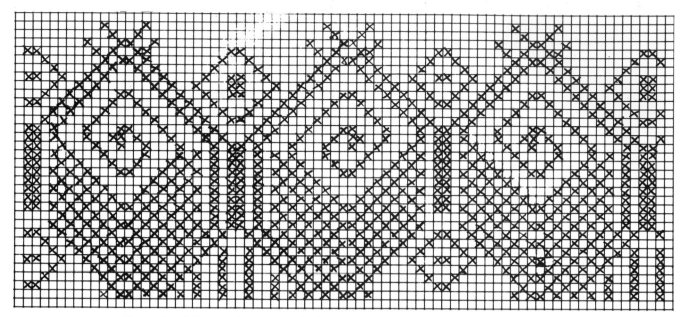

Elements of the previous three designs are combined into a more elaborate rendering. This also can become an excellent border design for tablecloth, pillowcase, towel, apron, and so on.

Ways of Repeating Simple Geometric Elements in Border and Overall Designs

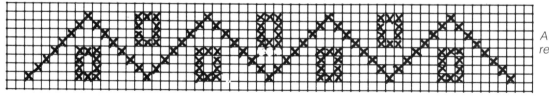

A simple zigzag and rectangle

Overlapping triangles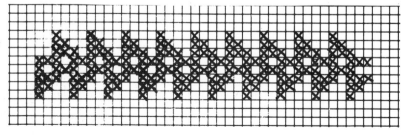

Single dominant units repeated with subordinate related units between them.

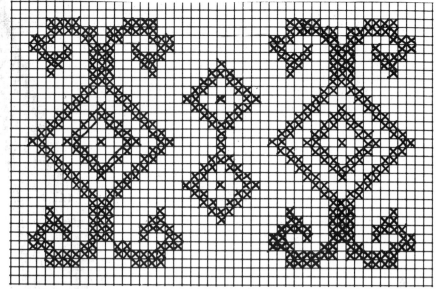

A diagonal grid filled in with squares to create an overall design.

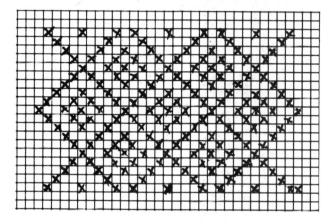

A variation of the grid and square idea as an overall design, with the interior square becoming more dominant by doubling the line.

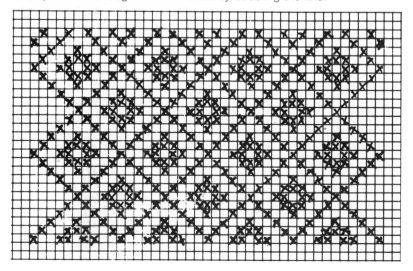

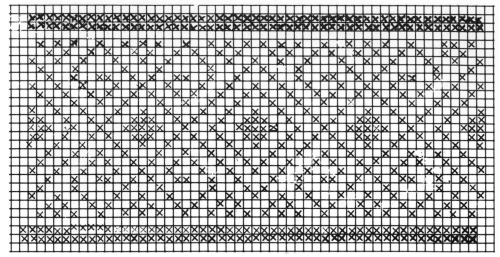

This border design utilizes some of the grid format and introduces the Greek key.

The grid and square idea is opened up more in this pattern, which can be adapted for either a border or overall pattern.

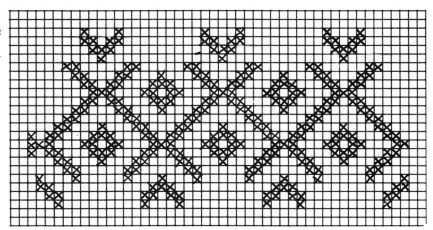

TRANSLATING DESIGN TO FABRIC

Once, transfer of design to fabric was limited to one or two ways. Now there is a host of possibilities. As many old ones as possible are explored in this book, and some new methods are introduced.

Before any translating begins, it is best to reinforce the edges of the background fabric or canvas. This can be accomplished by wrapping the edges with masking tape (or less preferably cellophane tape), by hand stitching using the overcast stitch, by running a machine zigzag stitch along the edges, or by drawing a bead of Elmer's glue along the edge and waiting for it to harden completely.

The background should allow enough excess around your design to permit hemming or mounting later. There should be at the very least two inches all around. If you are going to use a hoop, then the fabric should be at least four inches larger than your hoop.

Enlarging a Design

There is a simple way to enlarge a design if you have no equipment available to you. Superimpose a grid (lines as in graph paper) over your small design. Then determine the degree of enlargement. Draw another grid with the new larger dimensions and trace off the design, square by square. The final size will adjust in proportion to the original as you transfer the contents of each square in the new grid.

Another way to enlarge is to take a picture as a 35-mm slide of the design and then project it through a slide projector to the desired size onto paper or cloth that has been taped onto a wall. Merely trace the design following the projected image.

Tracing Techniques

Before any transfer is done, if your design requires centering in any way, it should be done at this point. You can determine the center by folding and then creasing the fabric or by basting a tack mark at the center. To find the center, merely fold the fabric in one diagonal from upper-left corner to lower-right corner. Crease it. Then repeat the operation from upper-right corner to lower-left corner. Where the lines intersect will be the center of the background.

Traditional Transfer Methods

Transferring a design to a background can be done in a variety of ways. (One not to be included is the commercial iron-on transfer. Little imagination or skill is required here.) All the following methods have been employed along the way in this book. We've all traced images from one surface to another using carbon paper. This is still valid. One can use carbon paper or dressmaker's carbon paper, which is cleaner than typing carbon.

Another method is to cut a pattern out of brown paper and then trace around the contours of the pattern.

Another is to use a counted cross-stitch chart (as found farther on in this book) and correspond grid-square for each completed stitch on tabby-weave (plain-weave) fabrics or on canvas. The magnetic cross-stitch finder can facilitate matching the paper design to your application by underlining each line, one at a time. It is quite easy to lose one's place, particularly when working on complicated patterns. When the grid or chart is used, it should be noted that the size of the chart has nothing to do with the finished size of the design. Sometimes the design translates smaller or larger, depending on the fineness or coarseness of the fabric background and how close a stitch comes to the size of the grid.

Another old-time method of transferring design to fabric is the pricking and pouncing method. Prick pinholes along the lines of the sketch and then pounce colored chalk through those holes, depositing it onto the background. When the pattern paper is removed, you can trace a more permanent outline on the fabric with pencil or a fine fabric marker such as the Nēpo marker.

Simple Tracing

One of the simplest ways of transferring a design to canvas is to place your sketch underneath and trace the design (that can be seen through the canvas) with needlework markers.

The completed checkbook cover. (Chart on p. 160.)

Using Dressmaker's Carbon

Another traditional transfer technique is to trace the design onto the fabric using dressmaker's carbon and then going over the lines with a fine-pointed needlework marking pen.

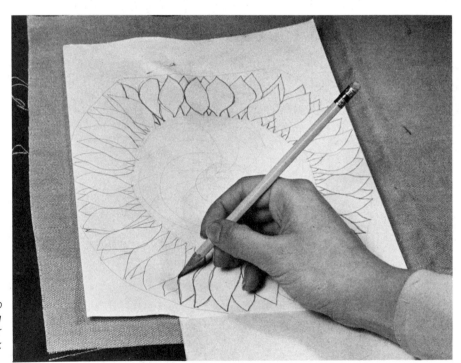

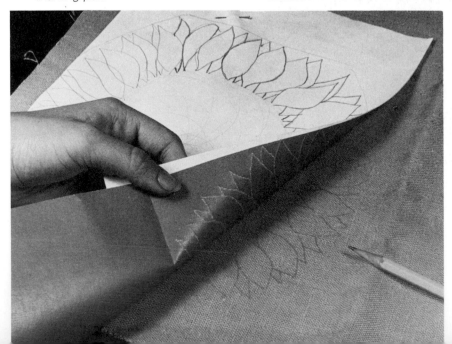

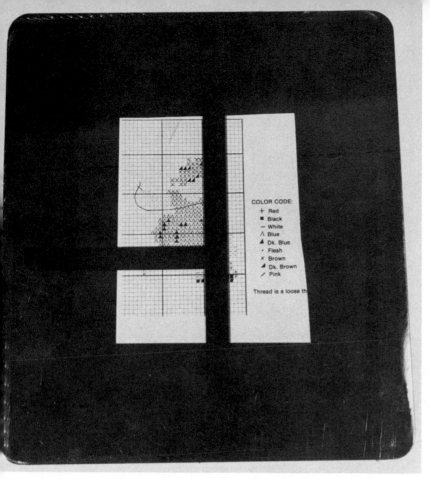

COLOR CODE:
+ Red
■ Black
— White
∧ Blue
▲ Dk. Blue
· Flesh
✗ Brown
◢ Dk. Brown
∕ Pink

Thread is a loose th

A magnetic cross-stitch finder facilitates locating the place where you are at when following a chart.

Using Waste Canvas

The original sketch.

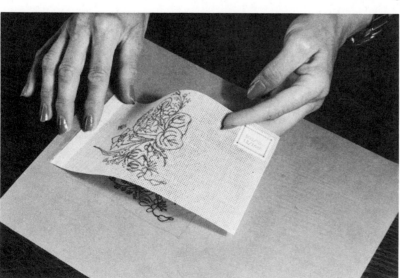

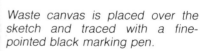

Waste canvas is placed over the sketch and traced with a fine-pointed black marking pen.

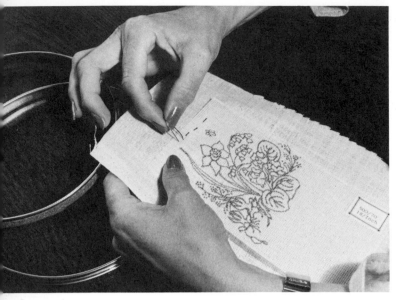

The waste canvas is basted onto a fine linen.

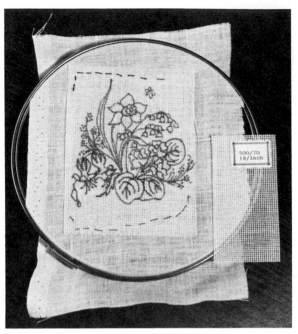

The design is ready for embroidering.

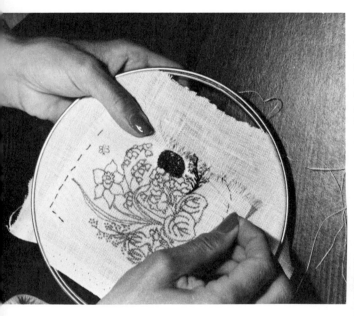

Embroidery is accomplished the same way as if it were done directly on the background. When completed, warp and weft threads of the waste canvas are pulled out leaving the embroidery "deposited" on the fine linen. With waste canvas, stitches can be regulated in size for consistency—or without an outline, the design can more easily be counted using a chart.

The completed embroidery utilizes several types of cross-stitches.

New Transfer Methods

Some more recent transfer methods are the use of transfer crayon or pencil, transfer papers, computer printouts, and heat transfer.

When transfer crayons or pencils are used, the design is drawn on a piece of paper with the crayon. (It is possible to use a translucent "tracing" paper and trace the design from another master drawing to the intermediate tracing paper using the crayons.) Then the design is ironed onto the fabric.

Iron-on transfer paper is cut into shapes, placed on the background, and then pressed onto the fabric with a hot iron. Usually an intermediary paper holds the paper parts in place and allows the iron to glide over the area without disturbing the placement of parts.

Heat transfer can be achieved commercially or by hand, using prepared transfer paper. Any printed image can be transferred this way.

The computer printout is another possibility. It is possible to take a picture, object, or person to a computer printout center (often amusement parks and shopping centers feature shops that have a machine and sell the service). A camera roughly photographs (scans) the person or object and translates the image into 22 shades of gray. Each value (light to dark) is represented by another typewriter symbol. If you assign a color with a corresponding value to each symbol, you automatically have coded your colors onto a grid layout (even though grid lines are not obvious). Complex pictures, such as portraits, can be done this way, as will be seen later on. The magnetic board here, too, will help keep a confusion of symbols "under control."

Another method that works when the background is translucent is to place a darkly inked design under the fabric. Both pieces are placed over a window facing into bright light or over a lighted television tube. The outline projects through the fabric, permitting the design to be traced with a pencil or fabric marker.

Using Fabric Crayons

A design is drawn with fabric crayons on paper and then placed over the fabric background.

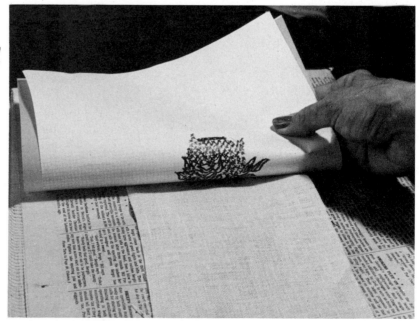

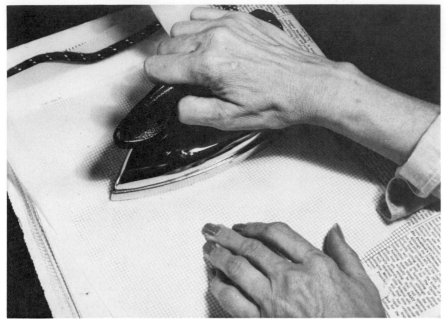

It is pressed in place with a warm iron.

The transferred design.

Using Iron-on Transfer Paper

A design is cut from the various colors of transfer paper and arranged on a background.

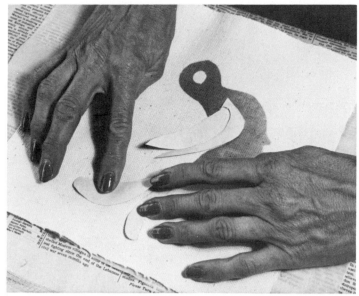

Each piece is turned upside-down on the fabric so that the color faces the fabric in its exact position.

Tissue paper is carefully placed on top of the design and fabric and then pressed with a warm iron.

The heat of the iron melts the color, transferring it onto the fabric and the paper pieces can then be peeled away.

The completed image is now ready for embroidery. These colors are supposed to be washable.

Something New: Ink Transfer

A color print is cut out of a magazine. These illustrated here happen to be daffodils cut from a seed catalog. The protective sheet of Fabulon is peeled away from the sticky plastic and the flower patterns are arranged ink-side down (the part you want to print) onto the plastic, making certain not to trap air bubbles underneath or introduce wrinkles.

The protective sheet is replaced over the flowers and sticky plastic, and with a squeegee that is furnished with the material, the piece is rubbed or burnished to make certain it sticks well and no air is trapped between the surfaces.

Then the entire piece is turned over and the burnishing procedure is repeated.

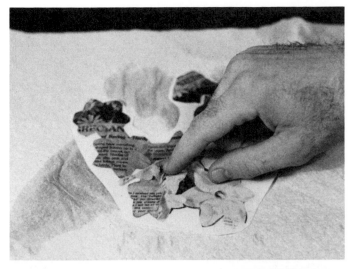

The protective sheet that is marked with the Fabulon label is peeled away and the flower-adhered-plastic sheet is soaked in lukewarm water for at least a half hour. The purpose is to soften the paper backing behind the inked surface of the picture. The thicker the paper, the more time is needed for soaking. If the paper floats to the surface, it may need to be weighted down with something.

After the piece is removed from the water, the softened paper is gently rubbed away with a finger until just the ink is left on the sticky plastic.

Excess sticky plastic is now trimmed away. And it is allowed to dry.

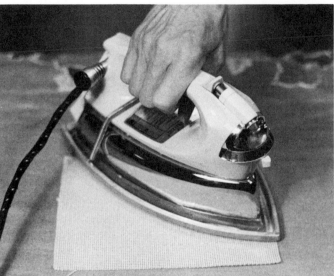

A piece of canvas is heated with a hot iron to prepare it for receiving the image.

Paper-side up (underside of inked image down), the pattern is arranged on the warmed canvas . . .

. . . and burnished into place.

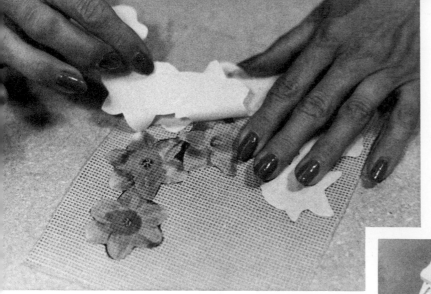

The paper is peeled away now very carefully revealing the ink that is now adhered to the plastic right-side up, as it should be.

With a hot iron, using a special protective sheet of paper (furnished with the Fabulon) for ironing, the piece is heated with as much pressure as possible. This causes the plastic image to adhere to the canvas.

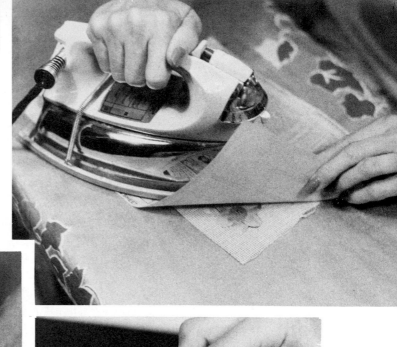

After the piece has cooled completely, the ironing sheet (which should be saved for other applications) is peeled away revealing a transparent or translucent inked image on canvas. The transfer process is complete.

Although the plastic also covers the holes of the canvas, a tapestry needle is sufficient to easily penetrate the plastic. As you can see, the holes are clearly visible. If the plastic pulls away, it is because it wasn't heated and pressed enough. And if you occasionally find the needle sticking, just dip the needle into water or spray with silicone. For some reason, water acts as a release.

Stitch as you would for needlework. Here I am working a cross-stitch, of course!

Something New: The Computer Printout

A paper shopping bag inspired this design. A computer printout image was made. A grid was superimposed over the computer sheet and also on the canvas to facilitate reproducing the design. The cross-stitch on canvas was begun.

With a grid, it becomes easier to follow and count out where each stitch is to go.

The completed needlework by Jay Newman worked in tiny cross-stitches using DMC Tapisserie wool with a brown background, and figures in beige, rust, and black.

The traced design is ready to use at this point.

In case your fabric is too fine to count, the design can also be traced with dressmaking carbon directly on the fabric—in this case onto a fine white linen. (See the completed piece in chapter 8.)

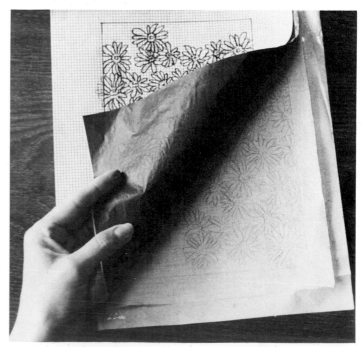

5
Basic Counted Cross-Stitch— A Focus on Geometrics

The very act of counting stitches presupposes a formal order that often results in formal symmetrical shape. It is a natural outcome and can produce an endless variety of designs. Most ethnic cross-stitch exemplifies this kind of geometric organization of space.

It can be simple and basic. It can also be more involved, as you will see as you follow the unfolding of design concepts in this chapter.

TIPS ON BEGINNING

Gather together all your materials—even-weave fabric or canvas, tapestry needles, yarns and/or threads—the total supply—material to bind the edges of fabric or canvas, scissors, hoop if necessary, and, of course, your design and the means for transferring it. Most items will fit into a plastic bag, which is easily transportable and, if you love needlework as I do, never too far from where you are.

You can ascertain if the size of your fabric is sufficient (allowing about four inches extra, two inches each way, for binding) by counting the squares of your chart, vertically and horizontally, as well as the warp and weft of the fabric. Choose a fine fabric or canvas for a detailed design; it works out best. A coarser weave should be reserved for bold designs.

Start your embroidery at the center, top of a figure. Follow the weave of the fabric. Begin by coming up in a hole, leaving about one inch of thread behind and securing it temporarily with your finger. Use your left thumb to guide the tension of your thread and fabric. As you continue to work the stitches, make certain that your thread will secure the beginning (end). Keep stitches traveling in the same direction by bringing the threads up and down each time for the same strokes. I usually complete the two operations for each stroke in one gesture—my needle comes up and down before I pull the thread to the proper tension. Keep referring to your chart or drawing. Most of the time the bottom stitch falls in the same direction as does the top part of the stitch. At the very least, there are always at least two strokes for each cross-stitch. Most often new stitches begin in the same hole as the last stitch. There usually is an interlocking of stitches, and, in some cases, none of the background will be seen. Take care to maintain the same tension for all strokes and for all stitches. Don't pull too tightly or allow too much slack (unless the design requires it). The thread should be the same size as the distance from the point of entry to the end of the stroke. To finish off the thread, or a color, run your needle under or through and over the last stitch on the back of the fabric or canvas. Cut the thread so that no tail is left. Start the next thread by running through at least three stitches on the back.

Usually it is best to start with broader areas of color and follow up with details last.

Where charts are given in symbols to indicate color, take care to observe where changes of color occur. For some complex designs you'll need to count very carefully.

Cross-stitch is a precise needleworking art. If you stab a stitch in the wrong direction or in the wrong color, pull it out by unthreading the needle and, with the needle, release the thread for each stroke (proceeding with last stitch first). Then rethread the needle and make your corrections.

If your fabric does not prove to be an even weave—this is sometimes true of linens and woolens—work over two fabric threads. You can check on the evenness of the weave by pulling out two warp threads and two weft threads. Another possible way to make a correction, if it is necessary to maintain the integrity of the design, is to work over two threads in one direction and one in the other direction.

You can also enlarge (or reduce) a design by working over more or fewer threads. Experiment for effects on a scrap of the same fabric.

If you are working on a border and need to turn a corner, place a small square hand mirror edge diagonally on the designed border, and when it appears to be angled correctly, draw a line along the edge of the mirror on the sketch, cut out the paper, and reverse the design with the diagonal matching and forming a miter (45-degree angle) at the corner—or whatever angle the corner is to become.

Some Do's

Buy the very best of all materials. You want your labors to last and hold up.
Buy enough supply of threads or yarns to cover the entire design.
Match colors in daylight.
If you desire washability, test your materials beforehand.
Allow enough excess around the piece for margins, mounting, or hems.
Bind the edges to prevent raveling.
When transferring designs, make certain your markers do not run.
Indicate the center of your fabric so you can properly place your design.
Keep warp and weft even (right angles) when transferring designs and when working.

Carefully choose proper thickness of thread and needle size to match the fine-
    ness/coarseness of the design and the fabric.
Cut your thread to about 18 to 20 inches long.
Keep direction of stitches the same (unless otherwise indicated).
Keep the tension even for all strokes.
If the thread or yarn stretches out into a thinner length, end the length and cut
    the excess away. This sometimes happens to wool.
Begin and end threads neatly from behind, avoiding use of knots.
When working on large pieces, fold or roll the fabric for easy manipulation.
When working on large projects such as tablecloths or bedspreads, baste the
    unworked or completed area into an old sheet to keep it clean.
Clip away large ends of thread or yarn on the underside.
Try to achieve unity of design by limiting color and kinds of stitches.
Do add your name or initials and date neatly and unobtrusively to the piece.

The original sketch for Connie Joy Newman's skirt.

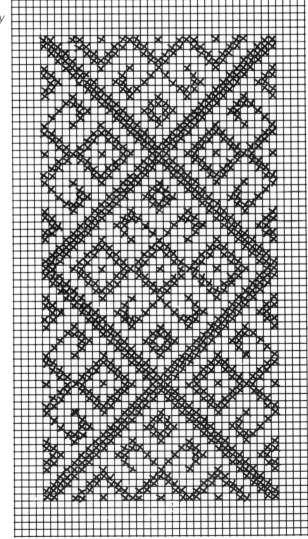

The chart of the skirt pattern. When there is a double row indicated, the cross-stitch is repeated.

X Light Turquoise
△ Dark Turquoise

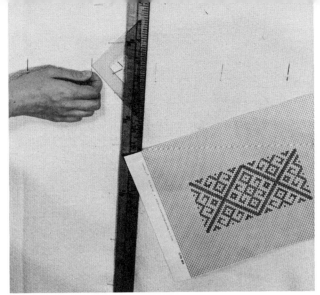

The pattern is carefully planned and centered on the white plain-weave wool of the skirt.

Pencil is used to help demarcate space division. This was necessary because Connie worked only from the small sketch. (The chart was done after the skirt was completed.)

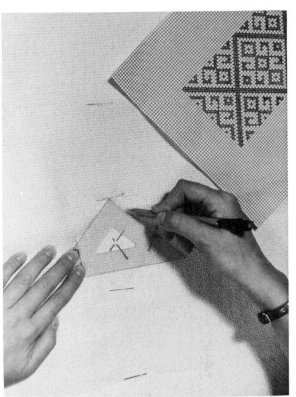

Simple diagonal cross-stitches were embroidered on the wool, counting out the design.

The completed skirt by Connie Joy Newman also has a part of the pattern repeated on the waistband.

Some Geometric Sketches for Counted Cross-stitch

These can be repeated as borders, as overall patterns, or they can be used as unique elements. Where edges look as if they should not become part of a repeat pattern, they can be deleted. Choice of color is up to you. The double row of cross-stitches in some of these can be interpreted with a more complicated cross-stitch such as a long-legged variety, a rice stitch, or a herringbone stitch.

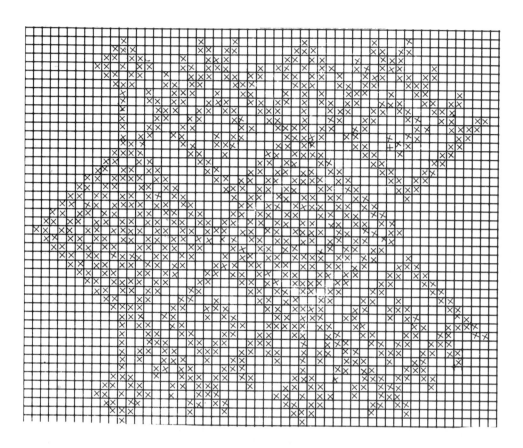

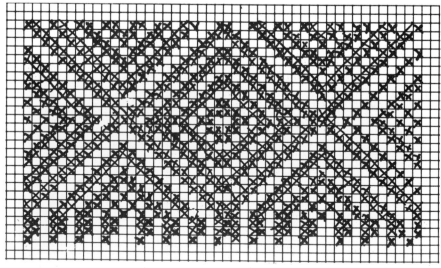

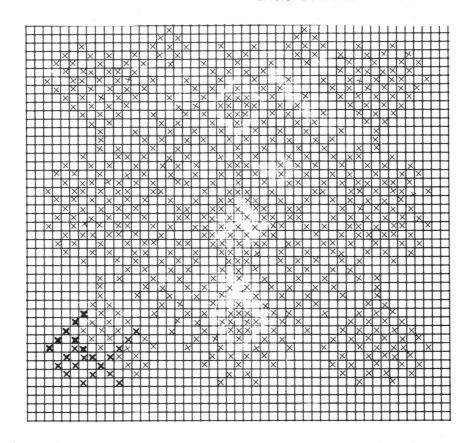

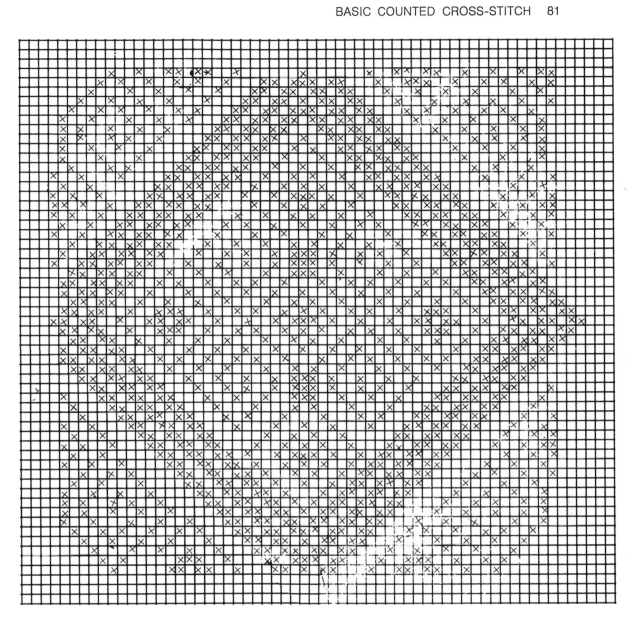

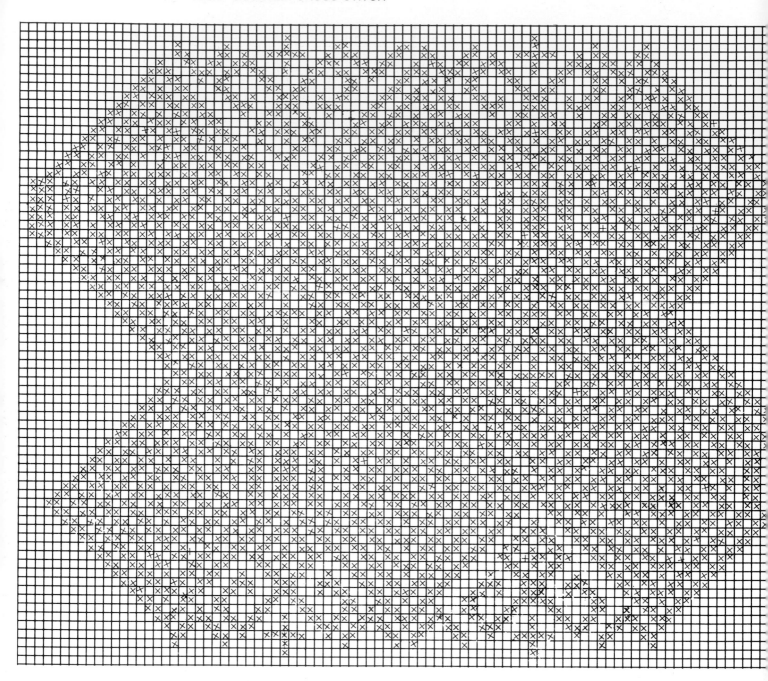

Translating Geometric Units to Fabric

Diagram for a napkin in diagonal cross-stitch.

X Light Color
✖ Medium Color
● Dark Color

The napkin on plain cotton.

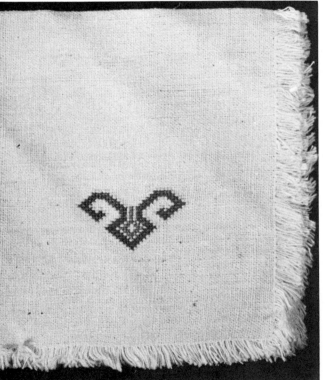

A close-up.

Diagram for a tablecloth that goes with the napkin.

◇ Yellow　　△ Light Blue　　– – Yellow
○ Violet　　• Dark Blue　　━ ━ Red
✖ Red　　──── Dark Blue

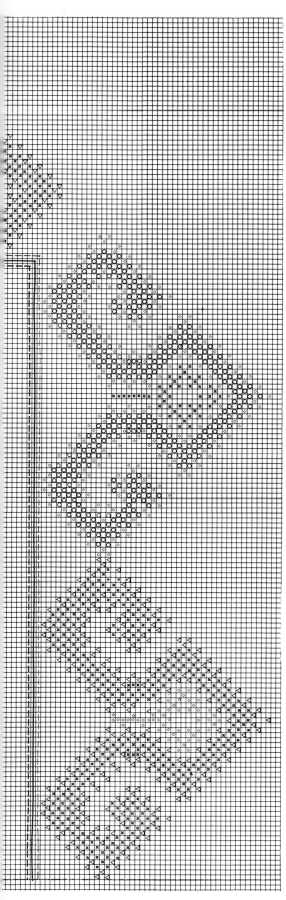

Geometric patterns worked in counted cross-stitch on a tablecloth.

Close-up showing pattern of tablecloth.

A basic alphabet of block letters for counted cross-stitch on fabric or canvas.

ometric design for a tablecloth.

usecoat with geometric designs embroidered in diagonal cross-stitch on a plain-weave tton fabric.

raditional Hungarian display towel worked in diagonal cross-stitch on linen.

hen purse of a sunflower worked in several complex types of cross-stitches. By the author.

Mexican peasant blouse in herringbone stitch.

Mexican poncho worked in diagonal cross-stitch in wool on woolen plain-weave cloth

A Cuna Indian mola inspired this insert for a leather album. It was embroidered on canvas using a diagonal cross-stitch. By Lee Scott Newman.

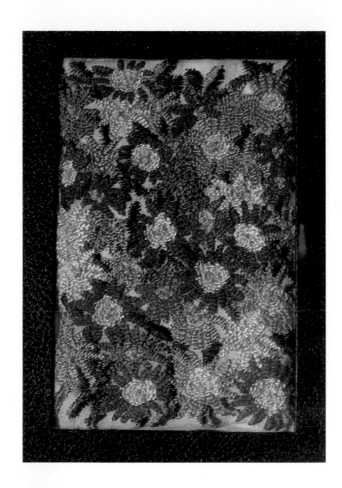

An address book insert worked in rayon on linen using the long-legged cross-stitch. By the author.

Self-portrait in gros point (cross-stitch) that utilizes a computer printout. By the author.

Wool on wool geometric pillow. By Jay Hartley Newman.

No Smoking sign worked with random and diagonal cross-stitch in cotton on linen. By Lee Scott Newman.

Druid rug worked in wool with diagonal cross-stitch on hemp.

Yao hilltribe (Thailand) pouch finely embroidered in cotton homespun and handwoven cotton.

Peasant blouse in the southern European tradition.

Sleeveless jacket from Afghanistan.

Panel worked in wool using a closed herringbone stitch.

Uzbek (Afghanistan) wall hanging worked in extremely fine diagonal cross-stitches completely covering the cotton ground.

Overall design organized on the diagonal in herringbone and vertical cross-stitch.

Geometric border design for placemat or tablecloth.

**Geometric Border for Placemat
or Tablecloth**

Chart for six-color repeat pattern.

✗ Yellow	△ Red	● Black
○ Green	✳ Blue	—— Black

Example of completed piece—cotton on linen.

Close-up of diagonal cross-stitch.

Decorative Nahuatlan Belt (Mexican)

Four charts for individual units of belt.

✖ Red

Example of belt with fine red cotton cross-stitch on white cotton with red wool tassels.

Close-ups showing details of the belt.

Small Sack

Chart for small sack (Nahuatlan)—the design can be repeated to enlarge the size.

✘ Red   ✖ Black

The sack is white cotton with fine red cotton embroidery. The tassels are red wool.

Close-up of the sack.

Poncho

Chart for poncho. The design is repeated. Two cross-stitches in a box indicate triple cross-stitches.

✘ Natural
✳ Natural
✘ Dark Brown
✳ Dark Brown

Poncho design is repeated. Colors are natural and dark brown wool on medium gray wool fabric. Fringes are natural wool. For poncho pattern see chapter 8.

Close-up of poncho pattern showing the linear aspects as negative space, with the background filled in. The stitch is diagonal cross-stitch.

✖ Black

Chart for border design that can be used for skirt, shirt, tablecloth, towels, etc. Pattern can be repeated.

Repeat pattern of black wool on a white cotton ground.

Close-up of pattern in triple cross-stitch.

Cross-stitched Quilted Bedspread

Individual squares are embroidered and then sewn together as in traditional quiltmaking. Square units are assembled. A filler of some kind is used between the top (embroidered part) and the back, which is the liner. They are then quilted together. (Individual charts are shown with close-up photographs. Some designs are repeated in the quilt.)

The single bed-sized bedspread is blue and white cotton with blue cotton diagonal cross-stitches on white.

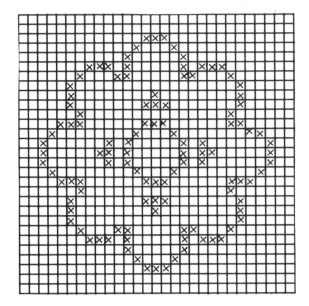

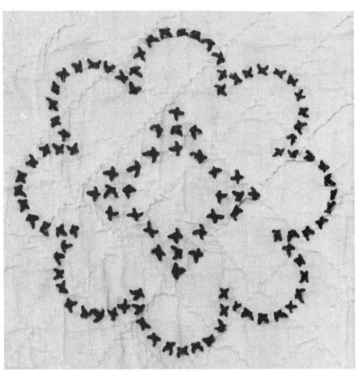

Some of the designs include French knots. These are indicated by small dots.

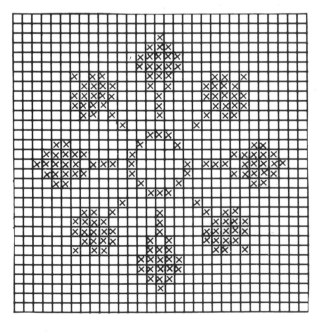

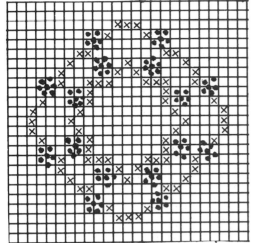

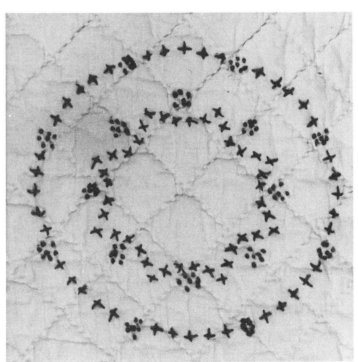

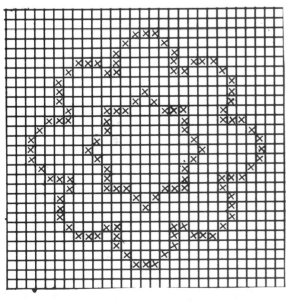

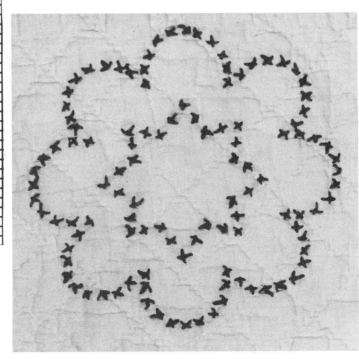

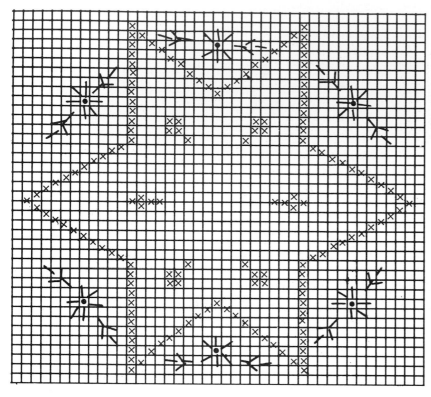

Straight lines indicate a running stitch.

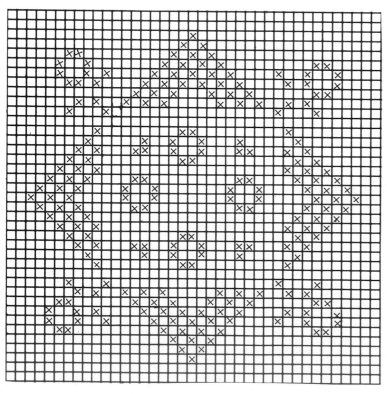
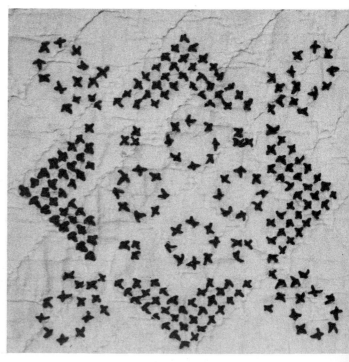

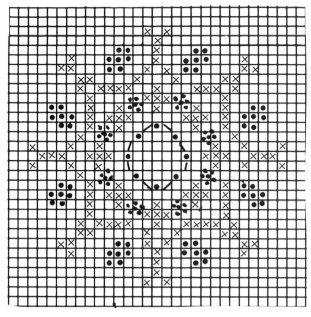

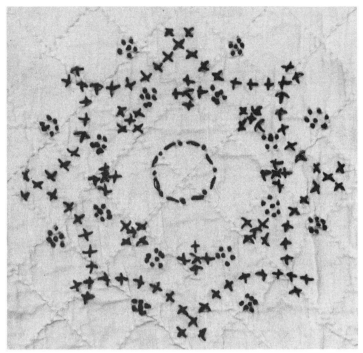

In these charts straight lines should be interpreted with a detached chain stitch.

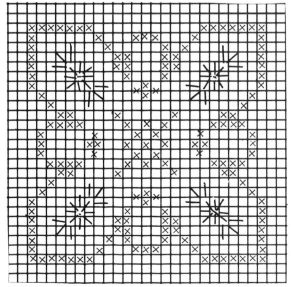

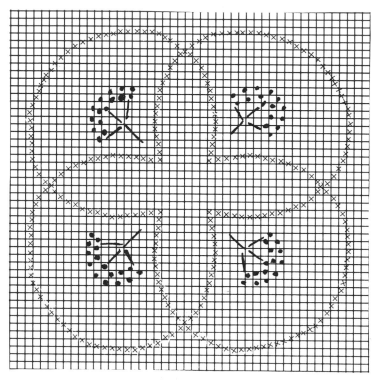
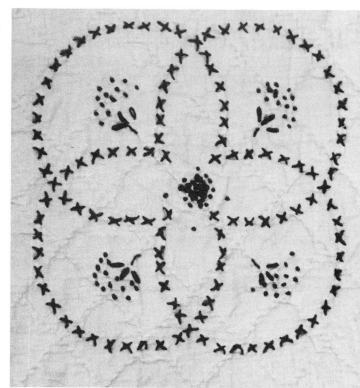

Straight lines indicate a detached chain stitch here too. Dots should be worked as French knots.

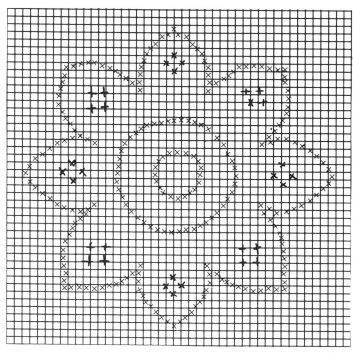

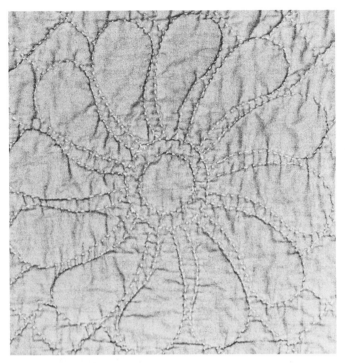

After assembling the three layers of the quilt, quilting is done in small running stitches in this floral pattern. Each square is stitched separately.

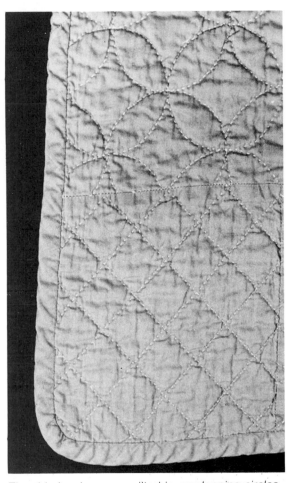

The side borders are quilted in overlapping circles.

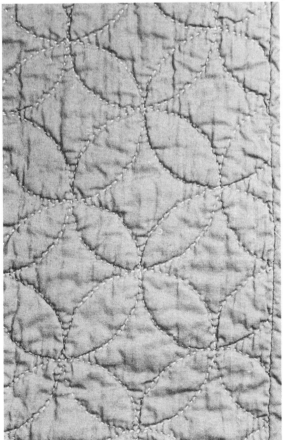

And the four corners of the quilt are quilted in a diamond (diaper) pattern, in which diagonal lines cross at right angles to each other.

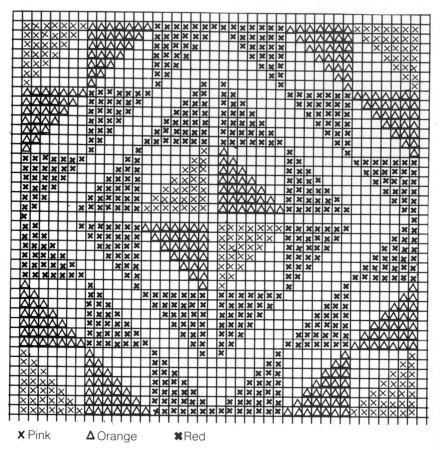

X Pink   **Δ** Orange   **✖** Red

Pillow

Chart for pillow design. The unworked areas will show up as the color of the background fabric.

The pillow is worked in diagonal cross-stitch in pink, orange, and red on a black ground. This cross-stitched unit is mounted in a red fabric.

A close-up of the Israeli design.

Housecoat

Chart for a design that repeats as panels down the front and sleeves of a cotton housecoat. The design units can be multiplied as many times as necessary.

ight	△ Dark	✖ Dark	
edium	○ Medium	● Medium-Dark	

The housecoat colors should be a combination of light, medium, and dark to achieve the effective contrast seen here.

A close-up showing the design closely worked in diagonal cross-stitch.

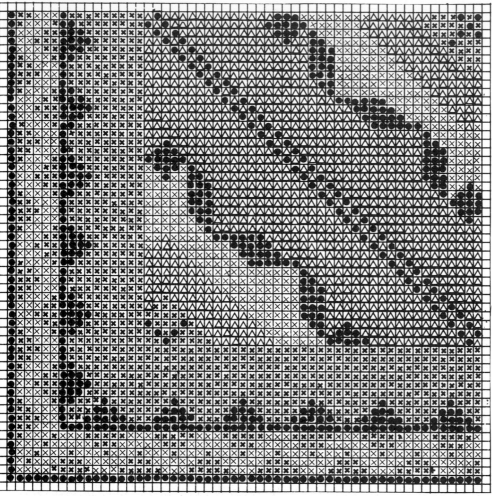

✗ Yellow   **△** Gold   **✖** Dark Green   **●** Brown

Two Druid Rugs

Chart for a Druid (Israeli) rug. One corner is indicated—the design is worked by repeating mirror images (a mirror may be used).

The size of the rug may be determined by varying the coarseness or fineness of the weave. This rug was worked in wool on a coarse burlap-type ground.

A detail showing the diagonal cross-stitch.

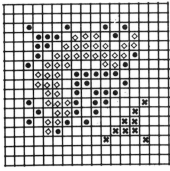

Chart of a repeat design for another Druid rug. This unit also represents one-quarter of a single section that will be repeated throughout the rug.

✖ Dark   ● Dark
◇ Medium

The rug is worked in wool on a heavy burlap background. Areas not indicated by symbols in the chart are filled in by weaving wool under and over the warp between the cross-stitches.

A detail showing use of the diagonal cross-stitch and the weaving of wool to fill areas not embroidered.

Fine Small Sacks

The designs on these small sacks or bags can be translated to other uses, both as single elements as shown here or as repeat designs.

✗ Light	✖ Medium	▲ Dark	▮▮▮ Medium	
△ Light	● Medium-Dark	—— Dark	– – Light	

Chart for a sack with an old design created by the Yaos of Thailand. Straight lines are worked in the outline stitch.

These attractive sacks cross-stitched in cotton on a homespun cotton cloth are used for storing silver bars—the favorite Yao savings plan.

A detail of the extremely fine and precise diagonal cross-stitches.

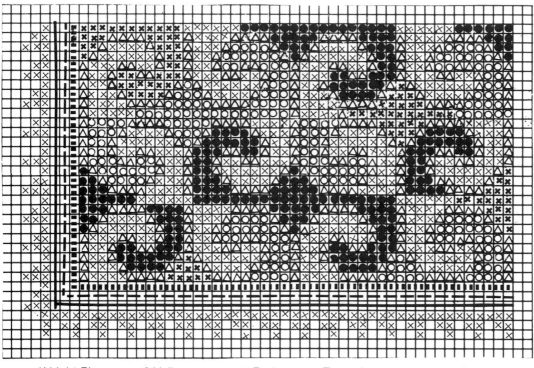

Chart for another Yao sack. One quarter of the design is diagrammed here—to complete it follow this section four ways.

X Light Blue   **O** Yellow   **●** Red   **IIIII** Turquoise

△ Green   **✖** Dark Blue   **— —** Red   **——** Yellow

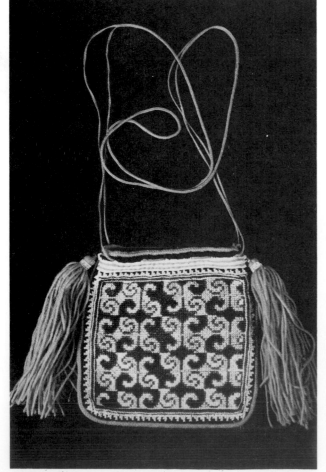

The cotton background of this sack is completely covered by cross-stitch. Straight lines are worked in the outline stitch. The design dates back hundreds of years.

A close-up of the fine diagonal cross-stitch and outline stitch. Tassels are of wool.

A chart for another Yao sack. Areas that are not filled with cross-stitch are rendered in light, medium, and dark values of the outline stitch.

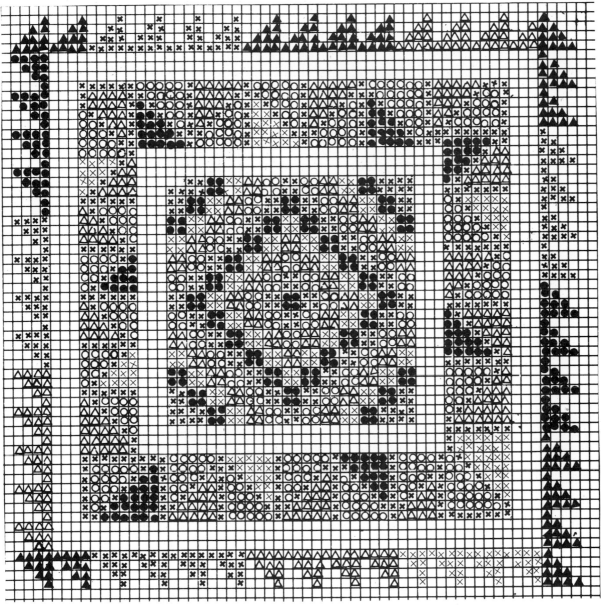

✗ Light	✖ Medium	▲ Dark
△ Light	● Dark	○ Medium Light

The Yao sack is another traditional design.

A detail of the closely worked diagonal cross-stitches.

Chart for a pattern suitable for a sack or repeat design. The triangles have been omitted from one side of the diagram to illustrate a repeat design possibility. For a single unit, stitch the triangles around the entire perimeter.

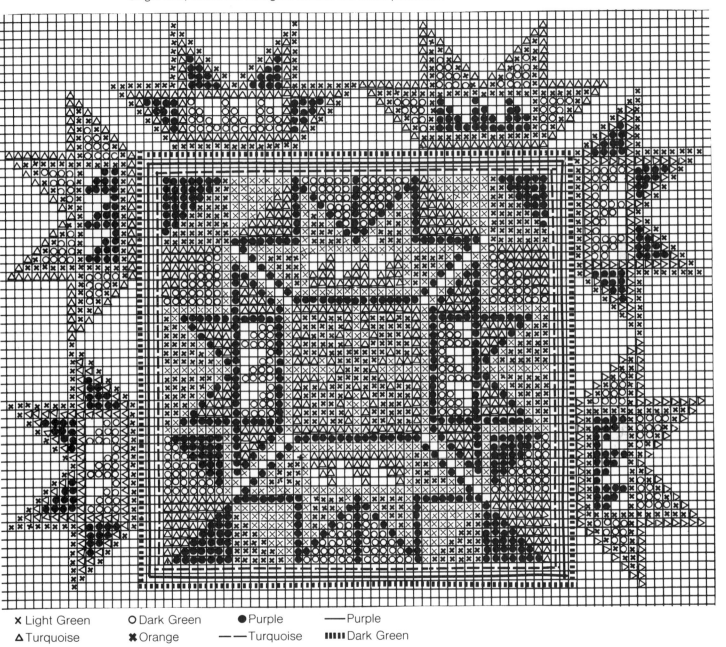

| ✗ Light Green | ○ Dark Green | ● Purple | —— Purple |
| △ Turquoise | ✖ Orange | — — Turquoise | ‖‖‖ Dark Green |

The design as a single unit cross-stitched in cotton on a homespun cotton background.

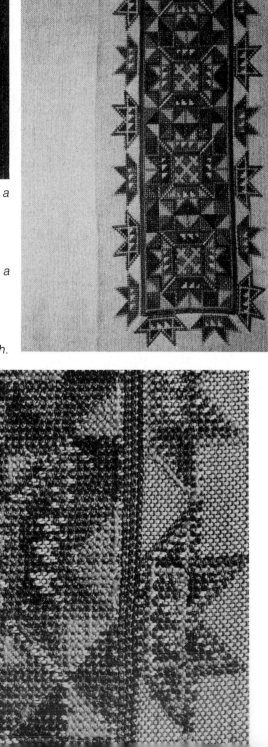

The same design repeated as a center decoration on a tablecloth.

A close-up of the tablecloth design in diagonal cross-stitch.

Chart for Uzbek sack (Afghanistan). Where the diagram ends, the pattern may be repeated.

✘ Light Green △ Pink ◇ White ✗ Gold

○ Dark Green ✹ Maroon ● Violet ● Brown

This very old sack was worked in silk using extremely fine diagonal cross-stitches so closely embroidered that none of the cotton background can be seen.

Child's Hat

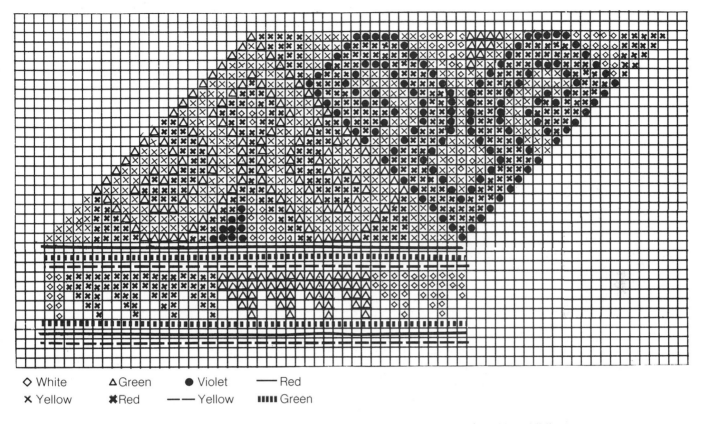

◇ White   △ Green   ● Violet   —— Red
✕ Yellow   ✖ Red   – – Yellow   ‖‖‖ Green

The Yao are a hill-tribe people of Thailand, and this is a chart for a Yao child's hat. The design may be repeated as many times as necessary.

The design worked in diagonal cross-stitch (without adornment) would make an attractive pillbox hat or a good border design.

Uzbek Wall Hanging

Chart for Uzbek wall hanging.

- ● Red
- ● Black
- ✖ Maroon
- ◇ White
- ○ Green
- ✚ Orange
- ✕ Yellow
- ✛ Gold
- △ Blue

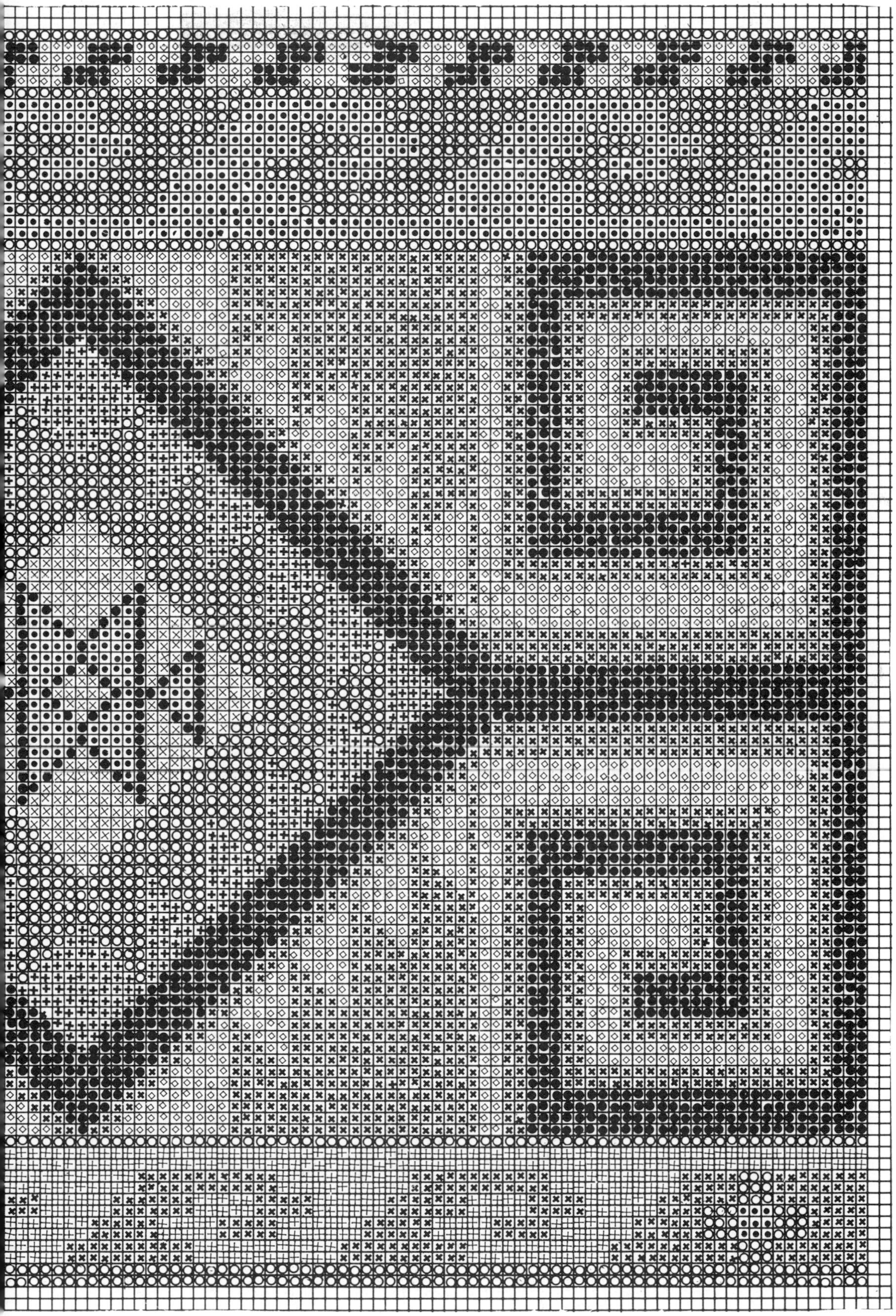

A traditional wall hanging from the Afghanistan-Russia border worked in extremely fine cross-stitches using silk on a cotton ground. The background is completely covered by the stitches. The tassels are silk as well.

A detail of the diagonal cross-stitches.

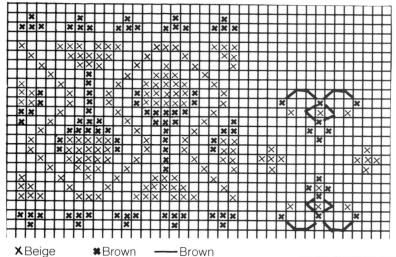

✗ Beige　　✗ Brown　　—— Brown

Two Southern European Peasant Blouses

Chart showing the two patterns that are repeated throughout the blouse. The straight lines are worked in an outline stitch.

The peasant blouse is made of sheer handspun and handwoven cotton with cotton thread embroidery.

Detail of a sleeve. Except for some use of the outline stitch, all of the work is done with thick thread in the diagonal cross-stitch.

The thread is so thick that in most cases only the top diagonal is visible.

Chart showing the two motifs and how they repeat. The second motif, indicated in straight lines, is worked in the satin stitch.

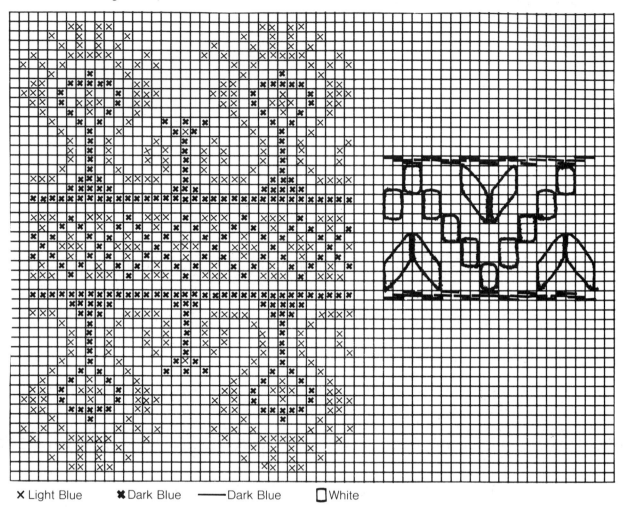

✘ Light Blue   ✖ Dark Blue   ——Dark Blue   ☐ White

The peasant blouse organizes and repeats just two elements into its own arrangement of stripes.

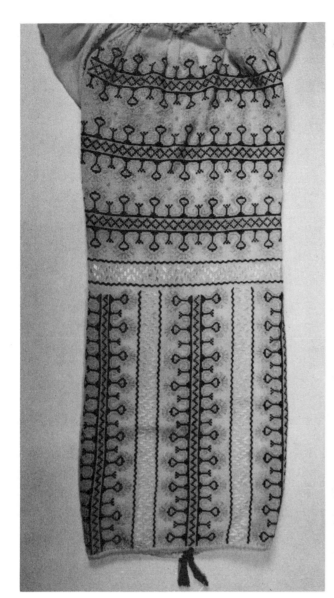

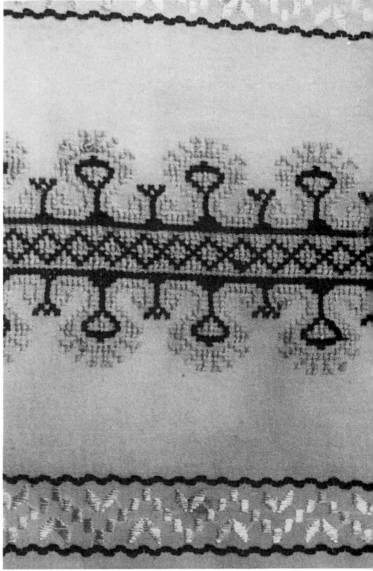

Detail of the sleeve showing how the motifs are arranged into patterns of stripes.

The embroidery is worked in diagonal cross-stitch using thick cotton so that, in most cases, only the top stroke of the cross is visible. The satin stitch is worked in silk.

A T'boli Jacket

Charts for a T'boli jacket.

✗ White   △ Yellow   ✷ Red

front

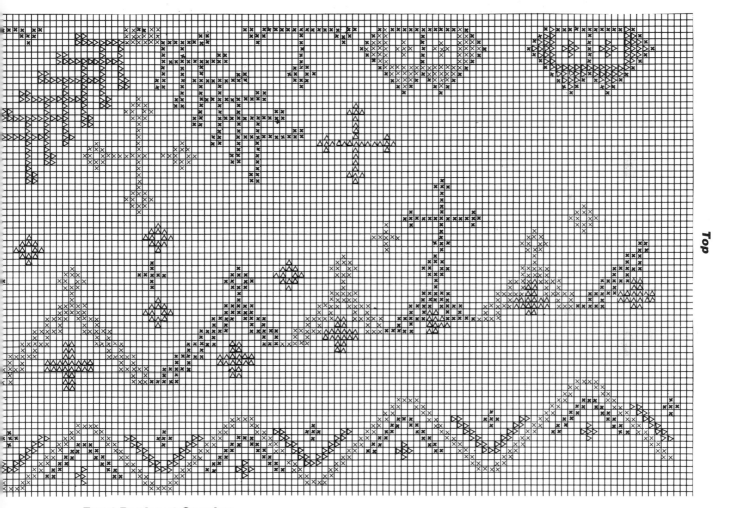

Front Border at Opening

Top

back

Bottom Border

✕ White   △ Yellow   ✖ Red

Top

sleeve

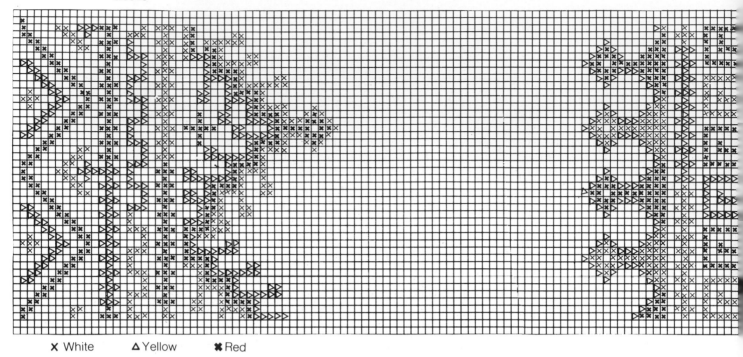

✗ White   △ Yellow   ✖ Red

The T'boli women of Mindanao, Philippines, wear these attractive cotton jackets (so does the author). This is a front view.

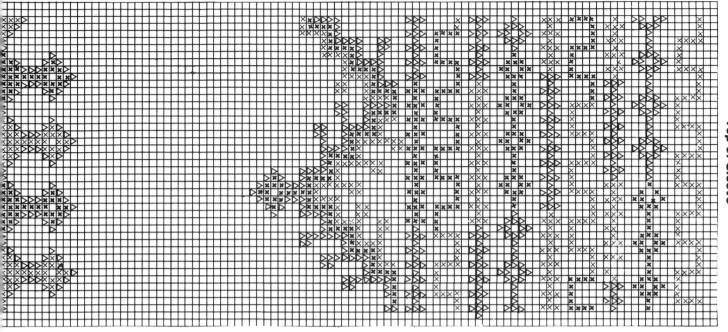

Top of Sleeve

This is the back view.

A Gallery of More Geometric Designs (without Charts)

A Mexican sack worked in wool on a wool background. The stitch is diagonal cross-stitch.

A repeat design in wool on wool using the diagonal cross-stitch.

Repeat design for pillow, tablecloth, etc.

Close-up of the diagonal cross-stitch.

Design for a pillow.

Design for a pillow.

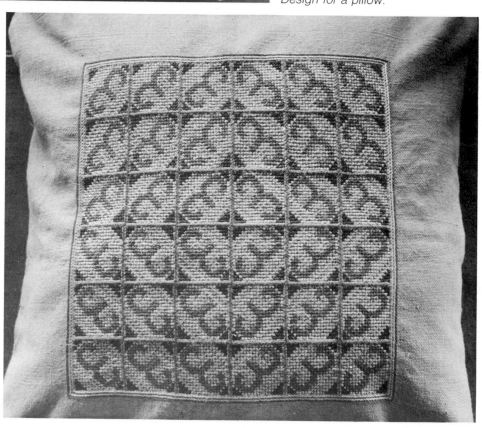

Two designs that can be worked as separate units or as repeats.

Three eyeglass cases.

6
Counted Cross-Stitch—A Focus on Stylizations from Nature

Although geometric styles of counted cross-stitch are probably the oldest design forms, the floral forms of Persia and the arabesques of the Middle East and central Asia inspired a flowering of natural forms from the Renaissance to the present. Fern, oak leaf, acorn, crayfish, dragon, rose, tulip, rabbit, and peacock are some of many old stylizations inspired by nature. In earlier interpretations, these are often repeated in the tradition of geometric design.

It wasn't until the late eighteenth century that the unique, naturalistic design became popular. Flora and fauna became less stylized and more realistic. Pieces became almost painterly in attention to detail and subtlety of color.

Here, too, designs throughout this chapter range from very simple renderings of nature to the more complex examples.

135

Some Latin American Stylizations of Human and Animal Figures

Stylizations can be abstractions when they abstract or select the essence of something without trying to literally depict it. Choosing essential elements, ignoring other parts, enlarging, reducing, embellishing, and minimizing are standard procedures for creating a personal stylization. Here are a few typical ones that appear in weavings and embroideries through many areas of Latin America. Some are interpretations of the human figure; others are of various animals seen from different postures. I'll leave it to you to imagine what is represented.

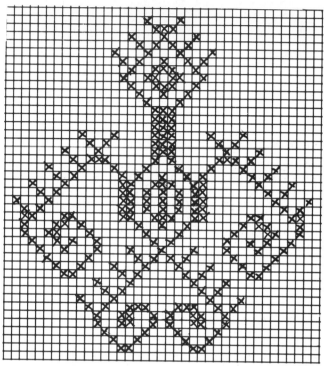

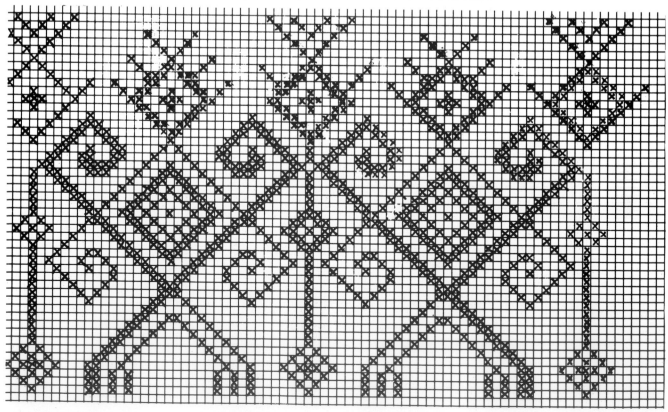

Even realistic scenes require interpretation when translated to fabric and worked with cross-stitch. Note that in People in a Boat *Ginnie Thompson leaves out unessential details.* Courtesy: Ginnie Thompson

In Piney Woods, *Ginnie Thompson carefully abstracts essential elements with a minimum of distortion. Note how she accommodates the wagon wheels to counted cross-stitch.* Courtesy: Ginnie Thompson

In the "Sampler" Tradition

Use of lettering personalizes and posterizes a message. It may express greetings, favorite sayings, or commemorate events. The sampler may also be a record of stitches, traditional images, as well as new ideas. Although the following pieces are not strictly "samplers," they owe their form to that tradition.

Ginnie Thompson adapted this piece from a drawing by Eleana Dewall Spriull. The quotation (used with permission) is from Wind in the Willows *by Kenneth Grahame.*
Courtesy: Ginnie Thompson

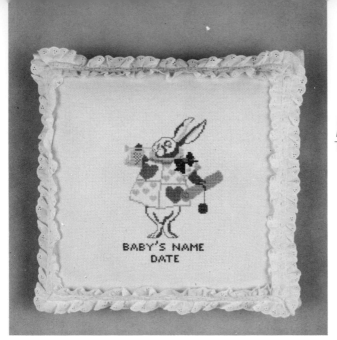

Here is a fine idea to commemorate an event. By Ginnie Thompson. Courtesy: Ginnie Thompson

Chart for a sampler by Lee Newman.

● Black ○ Red △ Orange ▲ Brown ● Black —— Black

The Sugar 'n' Spice *sampler is worked on linen with both rayon and cotton threads.*

A detail showing use of the diagonal cross-stitch.

Chart for Hungarian towel.

X Red   **✕** Black

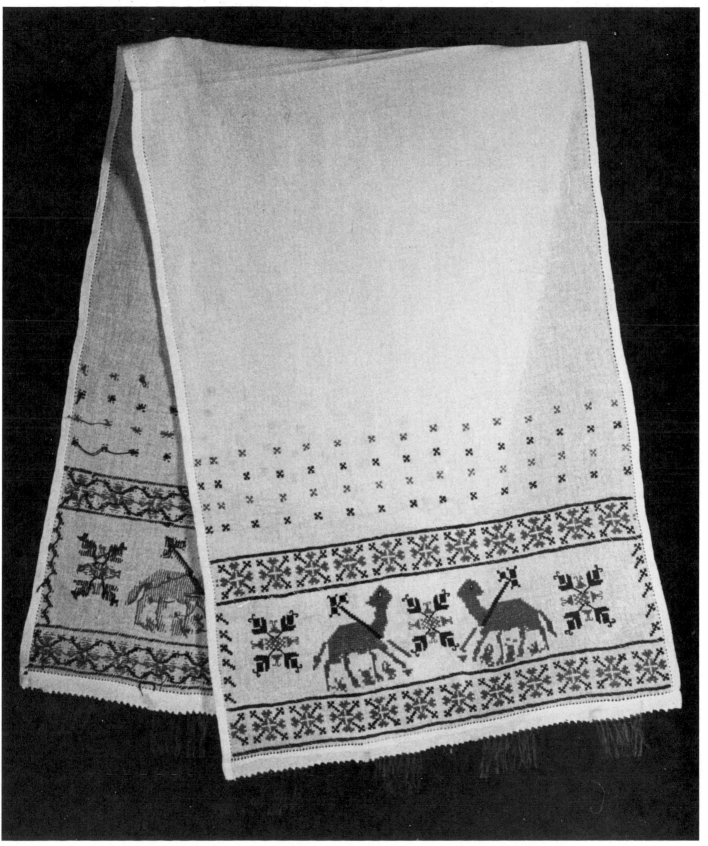

Although samplers are usually framed, the decorative towel was designed for display and not for practical use.

This chart translates into an oversized piece, but actually the work itself measures 15½″ × 23½″. (Please note that the design is held sideways in order to fit the chart on these pages.)

✗ Red   ✖ Black

Top

Center of Design—Repeat in a mirror image for the other half.

Another Hungarian piece showing use of geometric naturalistic symbols. The tree of life theme, central to this design, has an ancient tradition. (Chart on previous pages.)

Detail showing animal and bird figures prancing around the tree of life.

Detail showing closely worked diagonal cross-stitch. Lines are rendered in the outline stitch.

Three Sacks

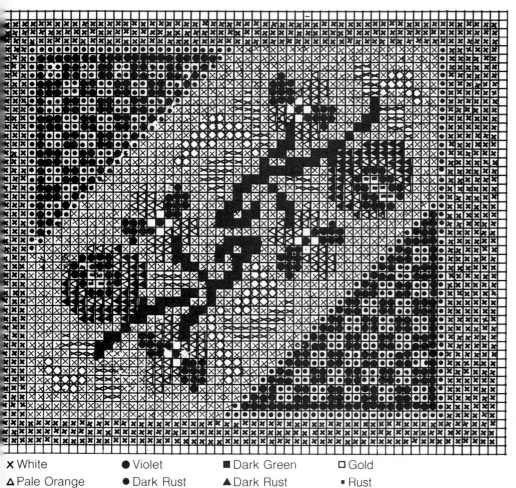

Chart for sack uses a wide range of colors. Every part is worked, as in needlepoint.

✗ White	● Violet	■ Dark Green	▢ Gold
△ Pale Orange	● Dark Rust	▲ Dark Rust	▪ Rust
✖ Black	✗ Olive	◇ Forest Green	

The sack is embroidered with wool, on woolen cloth, using a diagonal cross-stitch.

Chart for a sack in the Mexican tradition.

X Yellow Orange   ◇ Violet   ● Blue

▲ Light Red   ✖ Red Orange

○ Green   ◆ Light Blue

The sack is embroidered with a diagonal cross-stitch in brightly colored wool on black woolen cloth. Tassels are also of wool.

Chart for a sack that employs a repeat design based on floral and star elements.

x Red

This sack is worked in cotton on Hardanger cloth.
Pompons of cotton.

A detail showing the relationship of shapes and the
use of the diagonal cross-stitch.

Two Mexican Ponchos

Chart for a Mexican poncho. All elements are represented in this sampling. The design is repeated as many times as necessary to complete the piece.

✗ Red	✖ Green	▲ Pink
△ Deep Pink	● Yellow	✳ Blue
◇ Turquoise	◆ Yellow Orange	

The background is of plain-weave black woolen cloth with the design worked in brightly colored woolen yarn. (See chapter 8 for the pattern arrangement to sew a poncho. It is quite simple.)

Detail showing the use of the diagonal cross-stitch.

Chart for Mexican poncho/blouse detailing star and floral elements.

✳ Yellow   △ Violet   ✖ Red   ● Orange

The blouse is cotton thread on cotton. Floral and star elements are treated in a geometric manner as repeat designs. Colors are analogous: yellow, orange, red.

A detail showing the use of diagonal cross-stitch.

Pillow

Chart for pillow using floral images that repeat as a mirror image (as seen in a mirror). Just flip the chart around when stitching the opposite side.

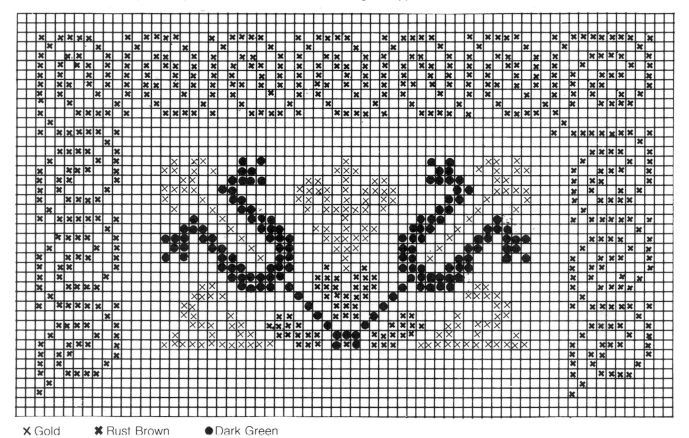

✗ Gold   ✖ Rust Brown   ●Dark Green

The pillow is worked with wool yarn on a plain-weave natural color fabric. The edges of the pillow are unwoven to create a fringe effect.

Close-up of the diagonal cross-stitch.

Table Runner

Chart for table runner. Two elements of the design are illustrated to show how units repeat—as many times as necessary.

● Fuchsia

＊ Vermillion

■ Blue

◀ Green

The table runner is worked with wool on a plain-weave natural color woolen fabric. The edge is treated in a natural fringe.

Scarf

Chart for Israeli scarf. The design repeats as a border as many times as necessary.

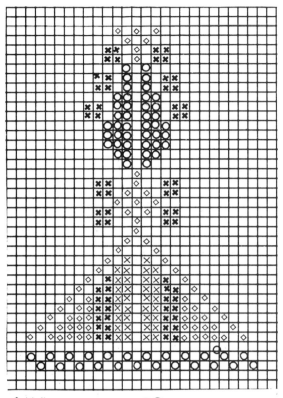

◇ Yellow   ○ Orange
✕ Yellow Orange   ✖ Red

The floral motif is worked in analogous colors from yellow to red cotton thread on a plain-weave dark blue cotton fabric.

A close-up showing the use of a fine diagonal cross-stitch as a border design.

Checkbook Cover

Chart for needlework checkbook cover as seen on page 58.

✘ Orange	✚ Light Green	● Black	△ Yellow
○ Medium Green	◇ Off-White	✖ Red	● Olive Green

Stylized floral elements in vertical repeat design.

Birds and flowers as collar and yoke of Mexican shirt.

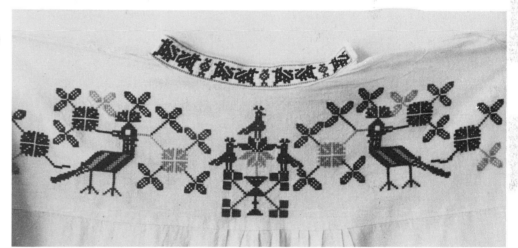

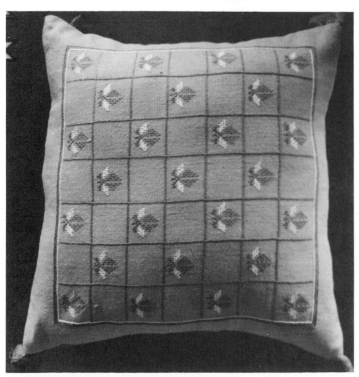

Leaf elements in a checkerboard arrangement for a pillow design.

7
Complex
Cross-Stitch

The cross-stitch examples described and charted here are not necessarily complex in design but rather complex in the use of cross-stitch variations—the stitch itself. Although certain effects are achieved using the needleworker's original stitch selection, other more simple cross-stitches can certainly be substituted. You would have to expect that the results will not be the same; nevertheless, in most cases, it will be as attractive.

It is best to experiment on a sampler before beginning.

Use of the Herringbone Stitch for Sack

Chart for sack that employs herringbone and vertical cross-stitch.

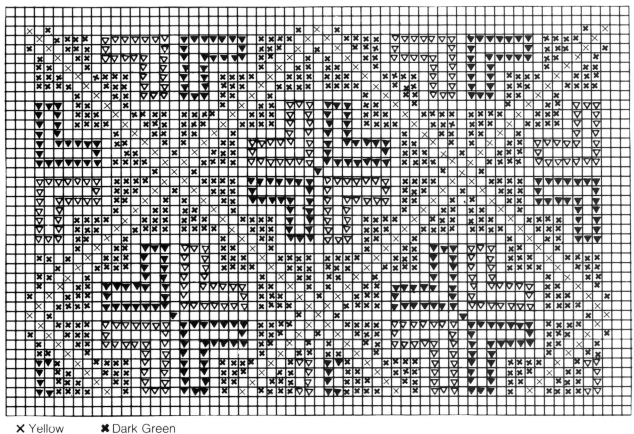

✗ Yellow   ✕ Dark Green
△ Yellow   ▲ Orange

The sack is made of wool with wool embroidery. Its essential pattern is organized with cross elements within a diamond. On closer scrutiny, one notices that the crosses themselves also form subordinated squares.

Detail of the herringbone stitch. The vertical cross-stitch is used only to demarcate the diamond-shaped units in this design.

For Ponchos

Chart for poncho.

✘ Gray
✖ Black

The poncho is worked with the herringbone stitch using wool thread on a heavy plain-weave cotton background.

Detail showing the use of the herringbone stitch.

Chart for another poncho showing the primary design element that is repeated throughout.

✖ Navy Blue
✖ Navy Blue
❘ Navy Blue

Bottom left: The poncho is worked in blue wool thread on a heavy plain-weave cotton fabric.

Bottom right: The solid areas of the design are worked in the herringbone stitch. Edges of the design are diagonal cross-stitch, and the Greek key sections are worked in the back stitch (an outline stitch is also practiced here).

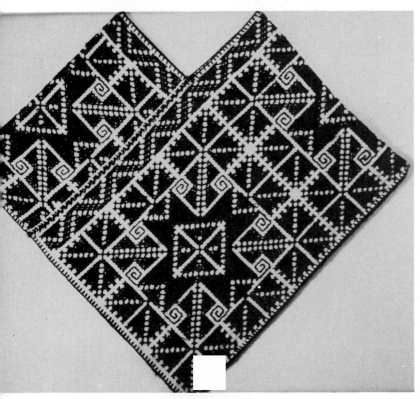

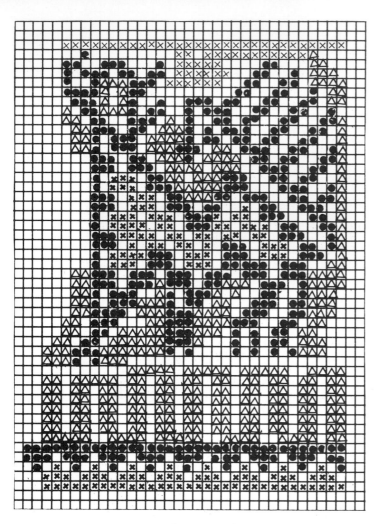

For Border Design

Chart for border design showing a single unit that may be repeated as many times as necessary.

✗ Light Blue
△ Red
✻ Green
● Dark Blue

A length of the border design is worked with wool thread on cotton.

Detail showing use of the herringbone stitch (albeit uneven and not too well done).

For Mexican Peasant Blouses

Charts for sleeve and neck areas of a Mexican peasant blouse.

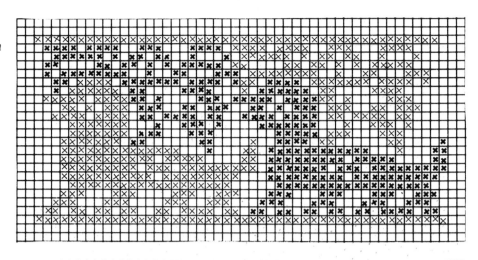

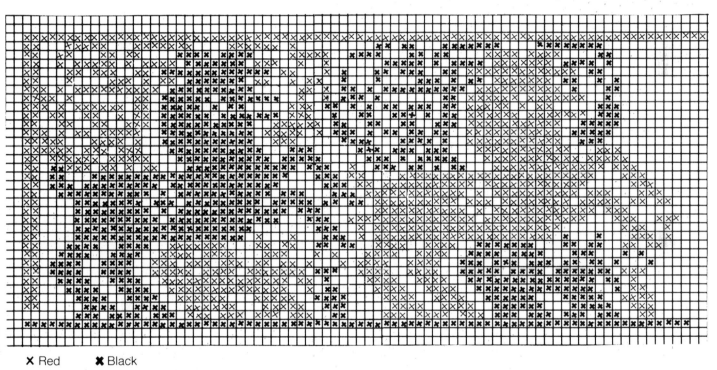

✕ Red   ✖ Black

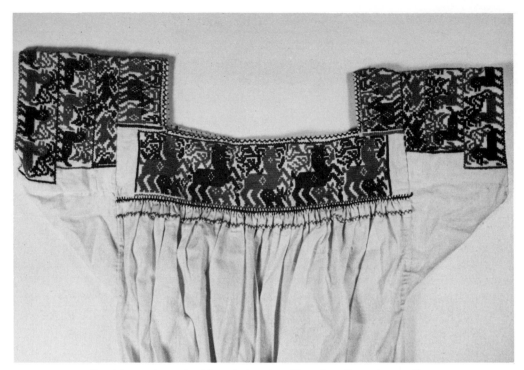

The blouse is embroidered closely with cotton thread on cotton.

A close-up of the herringbone stitch—so closed or closely overlapping that it looks almost like knitting.

Chart for a similar Mexican peasant blouse. The unit is repeated as often as necessary.

✗ Red   ✘ Black

This blouse is also embroidered in cotton on cotton.

A close-up of the tightly worked herringbone stitch.

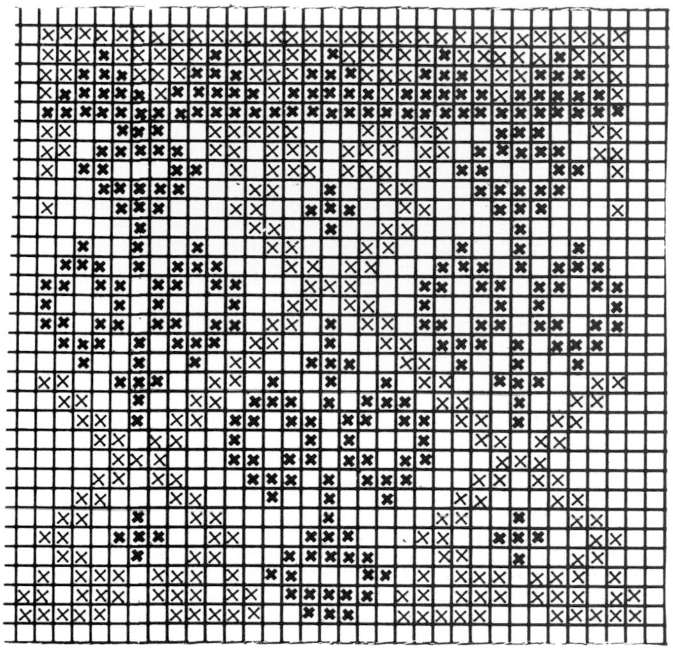

X Red
✖ Maroon

For Pillow

Chart for border design for a velvet pillow. The unit is repeated as many times as desired.

The design is worked in wool on cotton using a tightly overlapped or closed herringbone stitch. The center panel of the pillow is dark red velvet that picks out one of the thread colors.

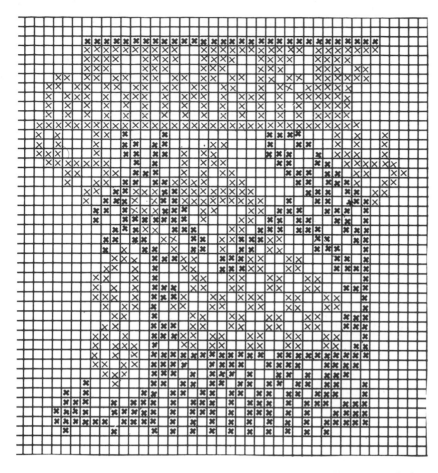

Chart for repeat design showing a single unit.

✘ Red
✘ Black

The repeat design is worked in wool on a Hardanger fabric.

A detail of the herringbone stitch and, in instances where a single stitch is used, the diagonal cross-stitch.

◇ Yellow   O Bright Red   ✖ Maroon   ✚ Brown   ∿ Yellow-Orange   ∿ Rust-Brown

✗ Orange   ● Lavender   ● Gray   ∿ Red   ∿ Rose

For Bedspread

Opposite page: Chart for a bedspread.

The bedspread is of heavy creamy white plain-weave wool with wool yarn used to embroider the tree of life design.

A photograph of the entire single-bed bedspread, showing that the design of the central section is the same in each half—a mirror image.

A single unit.

Detail showing the use of the closed herring-bone stitch and also the diagonal cross-stitch.

Another detail showing the use of the closed herringbone stitch.

Detail showing the closed herringbone stitch and, within the bird, the wave stitch.

Another detail showing the use of the closed herringbone stitch, and the wave stitch within the star petals.

For Wall Hanging

Chart for wall hanging—a fantasy scene of animals and birds from Mexico.

X Light Pink
◇ Medium Pink
O Rose
△ Dark Red
✖ Medium Red
● Dark Maroon
—— Dark Red

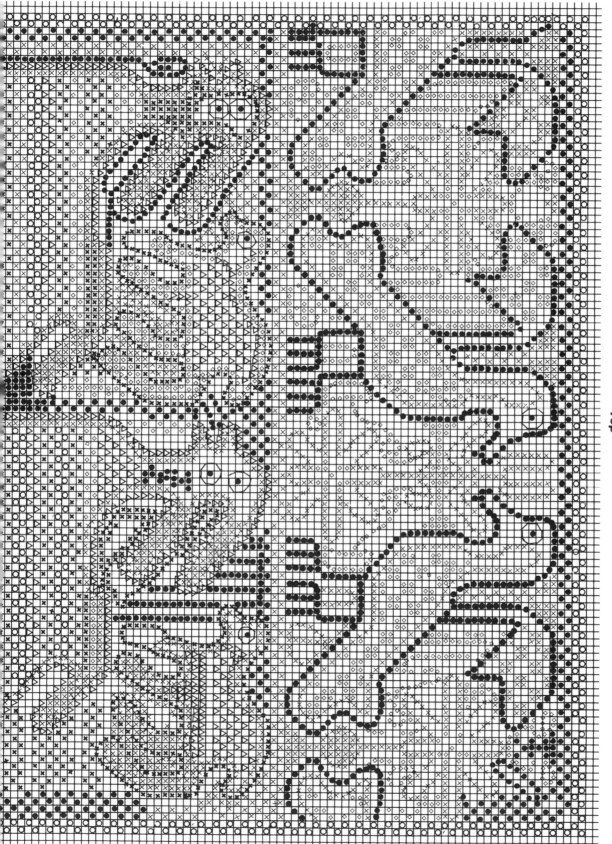

Top

The wall hanging is worked with wool yarn on a coarse cotton background.

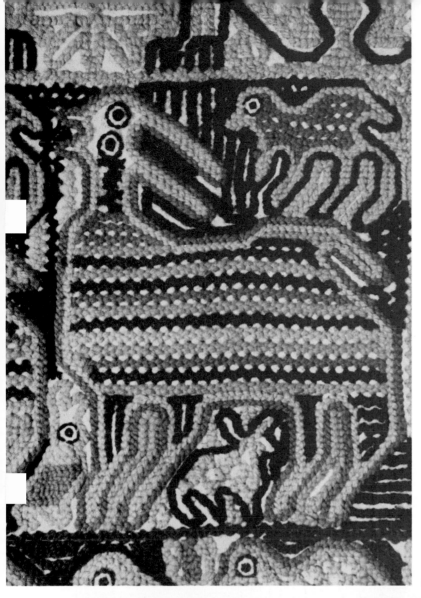

Two detail views of the closed herringbone stitch.
Eyes are defined with an outline stitch.

"No Smoking" Sign

Chart for Lee Newman's "No Smoking" Sign. The smoke is a random cross-stitch rendered in overlapping curves.

◇ White   ● Red   ⅄⅄ White
● Gray   ⅄⅄ Gray

Except for the smoke, the entire piece is worked using cotton thread in diagonal cross-stitch on a linen fabric. The smoke is worked using the random cross-stitch.

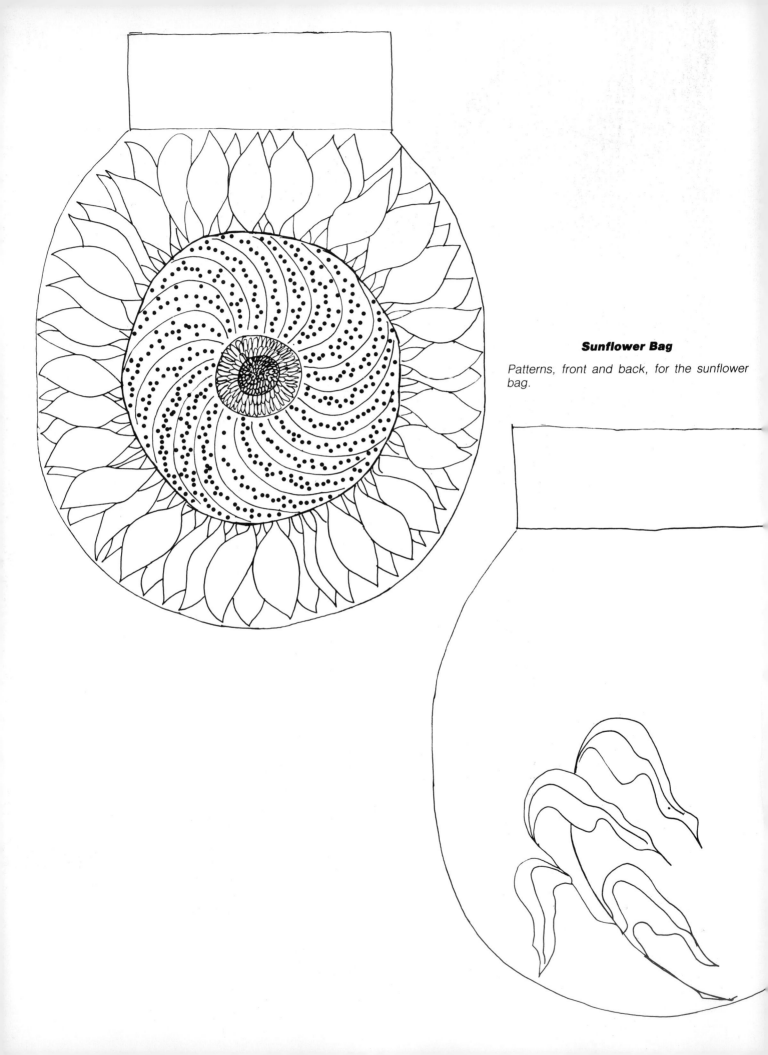

Sunflower Bag

Patterns, front and back, for the sunflower bag.

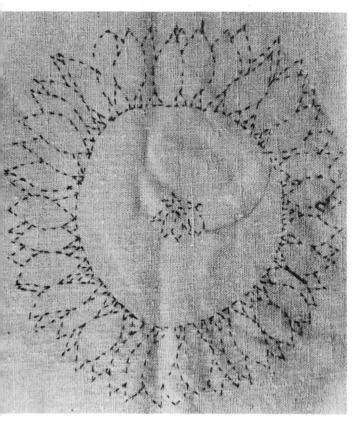

The patterns are traced onto the linen using dressmaker's carbon and are then followed using a basting stitch. The basting stitch will be removed later (after serving as a guideline) when the embroidery has been completed.

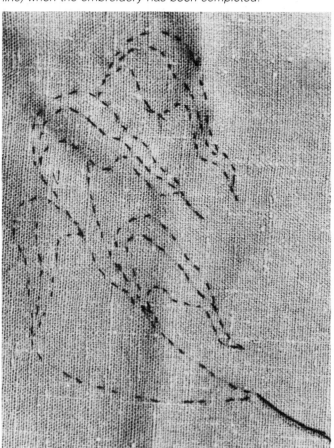

The embroidery in progress, showing several stitches in different stages of completion. At the center is the Astrakhan velvet stitch. This is worked in rayon. The petals are worked in two colors of pearl cotton using cotton pearl thread. And the center section is created using a combination of Smyrna (in two colors of green-brown rayon) with French knots of cotton pearl superimposed in a radiating design. The making of the rest of this purse can be seen in chapter 8.

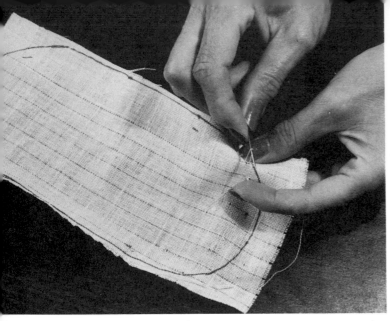

Since the entire background will be covered, measuring and counting is facilitated by pulling threads to form a grid. The fabric is white linen.

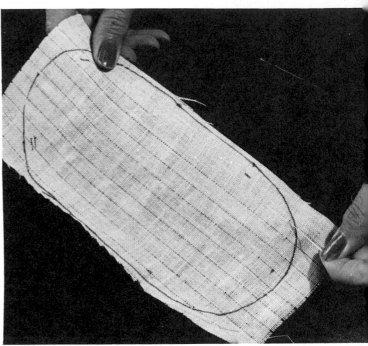

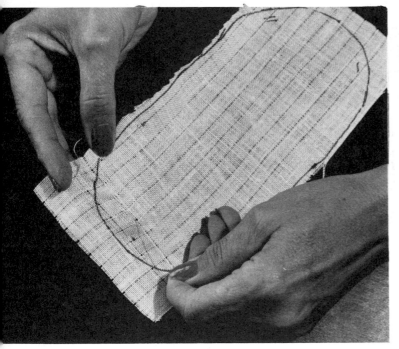

Two stages of working the large diagonal cross-stitch with straight cross variation. It was rendered in two colors of wool—rust and maroon. The opposite side of the eyeglass case was done in the Smyrna cross-stitch (double cross-stitch). See chapter 8 for the completion of this eyeglass case. (See pages 193–94.)

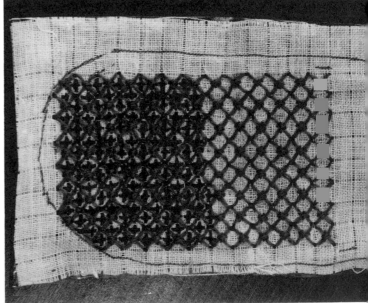

In India, the long-legged cross-stitch is popularly used as a filling stitch. Most of the fill-in work on this wall hanging was done in silk thread on cotton using the long-legged cross-stitch.

Some Uncharted Pieces That Utilize Complex Cross-stitches

Two close-up sections of the wall hanging showing stitch detail.

Two more Mexican wall hangings that utilize the closed herringbone stitch. These are worked in wool on woolen cloth.

Skirt top and detail showing use of the closed herringbone and the diagonal cross-stitch.

8
Finishing:
Blocking
and Mounting

After completing the embroidery, don't forget to add your name or initials and the date in cross-stitch or outline stitch.

Dry-clean your work, particularly if it is made of wool, or if the piece is soiled and the colors are water-fast and will not bleed, wash the piece in cold water with cold water liquid soap (Woolite). If the dye later appears to run, dip the piece into vinegar and cold water and then rinse it until the water runs clear. Rinse well (don't wring it out). One-quarter cup of white vinegar in one quart of cold water tends to brighten threads and whiten yarns. Hand-squeeze the piece and roll it in a towel to absorb excess moisture. As soon as the piece is damp and not dripping wet, place the embroidery facedown on a soft, padded surface (this keeps the stitches from flattening) and press on the back with a steam iron, if available, or regular iron until dry.

BLOCKING

If the piece looks uneven or puckered, then pull the fabric, while pressing it, so that the warp and weft return to right angles.

Even if the finished piece is not dirty, it should be dampened and pressed or blocked on the back, starting from the center and pressing out toward the edges. If the work is badly out of shape, dampen it and tack it onto an aluminum-foil-covered

188

piece of Celotex or soft-wood board, using aluminum pushpins. (Steel pins may rust.) Start at one end and stretch it taut while tacking the piece along the left and then along the bottom and up the right side with pins. Allow it to dry while tacked in place.

Some needleworkers spray the pressed piece with spray starch.

Keep finished pieces out of the sun and away from heat.

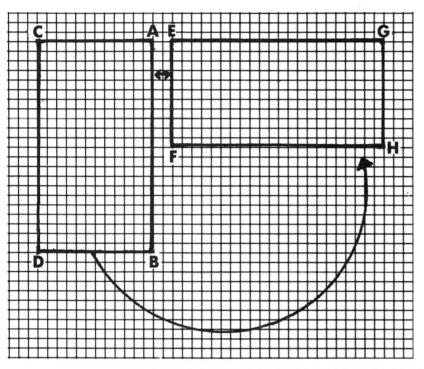

Making a Poncho

Two poncho patterns are shown here representing both a small size for children and small adults and a larger size for adults. Each piece of the small size is 12″ × 22″ and of the large one, 18″ × 34″. The scale is 10 squares to the inch. It is quite simple to construct each poncho—the pieces are attached at the points indicated by arrows. A and E meet to form a straight line between C and G, and F meets line AB at its center. D and H are then brought together with B meeting line HF at its center. After being assembled, the poncho can be folded into a triangle and worn that way, or it can be worn with front and back sides as straight edges.

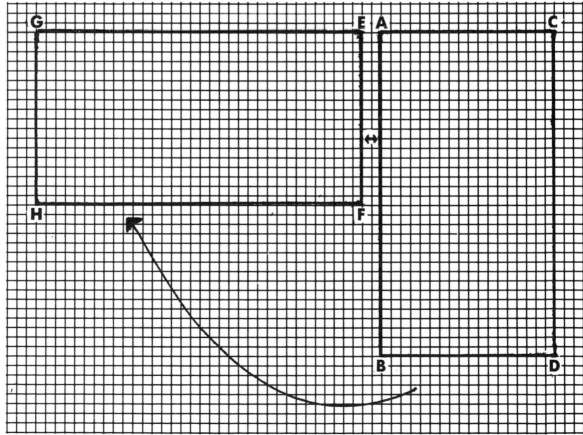

Poncho (shown again) with triangular folding.

FRAMING

Canvas pieces can be used for upholstery, sides of purses, or shopping bags, tennis covers, etc., or they can be framed. If they are stretched and framed, do not use them under glass. Sometimes cotton and wool seem to "sweat" under glass, resulting in a wrinkling of the piece with a wavy or corrugated effect forming.

When a piece is being mounted on a board for framing, white glue can be run along the back edge of the board and along the edge of the piece, and both can be held in place with clip-type clothespins until the glue sets. Excess fabric can then be trimmed away.

Another method is to wrap the board with soft white cotton fabric (a clean old sheet) and sew the sheet snugly in place so that the board is completely enclosed, then stitch your fine needlework to the cloth, stretching the piece taut as you whip-stitch it along the edges.

Mounting a Hanging

After a preliminary dampening and stretching while the linen sampler is being pressed (showing a range of complex cross-stitches), a sheet of one-sided stick-on Pellon was pressed onto the back to give the piece body and hold stitches firmly in place. Two-sided stick-on Pellon was used to fold back and secure the edges (instead of stitching). This creates a seamless edge.

190

The metal rod that comes with the ready-made bamboo stick is placed at the top (and then bottom), and two-sided sticking Pellon is pressed in place at both ends.

The rods are threaded through rings in the bamboo, ball screws are screwed in place, and the piece is ready for hanging.

Still another way to stretch and frame a piece is to sew threads along the back, attaching all sides as if you were lacing it. Thread-tension pulls edges tightly around the board. I prefer the stitching methods (rather than gluing) because the work can later be removed and cleaned.

Frames can be custom-made of leather as described here in making an album.

Mounting Lee Newman's "No Smoking" Sign

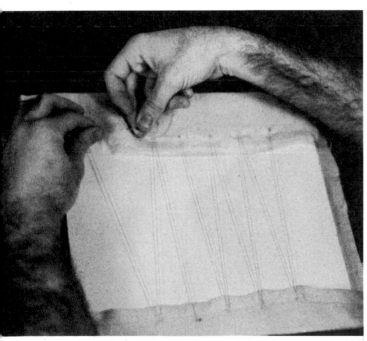

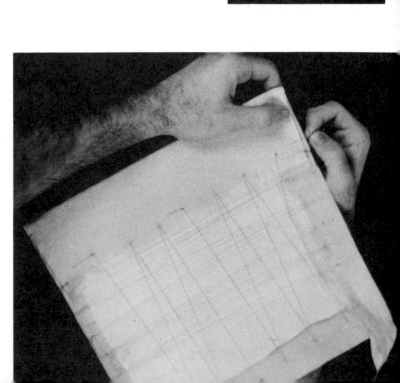

Nylon fishing line is laced through all sides of the piece and pulled taut over a foam-core board (a commercial mounting board sandwich of styrene foam between paper). Be certain that the piece is properly pressed first and centered the way you want it on the front of the board. Lace one side and then the other. Edges are neatly tucked under and stitched closed using an invisible hemming stitch (overcast stitch).

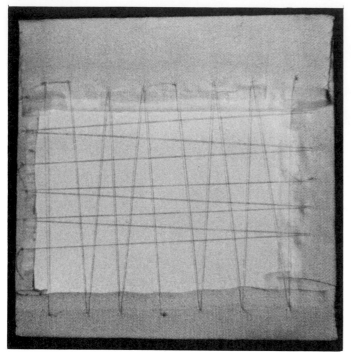

When the piece is completely laced, it should be taut, flat, and removable for future cleaning, if necessary. See chapter 7 for the completed piece.

Stretching a Needlework Piece

After being steamed and stretched during pressing, the needlework is centered over an oil-painting stretcher. It is then stretched as one would stretch canvas. The fabric is drawn over the stretcher with a canvas stretcher (see left hand) and attached with wire staples propelled by a heavy-duty stapler (see right hand). Begin with the top center, then tack the bottom, left and right sides. Work your way toward the corners while pulling the canvas taut—but not enough to tear it.

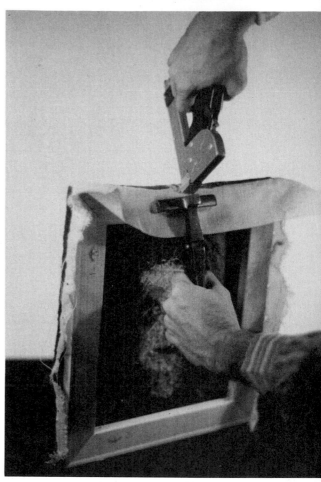

When it is completed, tuck in the corners neatly forming a miter and tack in place. Then cut away excess. The completed, framed portrait can be seen in the color section.

MOUNTING NEEDLEWORK AS PURSE, EYEGLASS CASE, ETC.

I find that after blocking a work, attaching iron-on Pellon to the back of the embroidery acts as a moderate stiffener and also holds stitches in place for hard-wear items such as purses and eyeglass cases.

A simple way to make an eyeglass case is to cut your pattern after estimating the proper shape and size to accommodate your glasses. Trace this pattern along your needlework (if you haven't done this already) and then trim. Repeat the operation, cutting out the stiffener (interlining) and lining fabric. With right side facing in and wrong side out, sew the needlework, interlining, and lining together along the edges, allowing an opening so that each part can be turned inside out. After stitching together, return the sides right side out and blind-stitch the open edge. Then, using a decorative stitch, attach the two sides together, leaving an opening at the top so that glasses can be slipped into the case.

Making an Eyeglass Case

Using a pattern made by measuring the eyeglass sizes, a line was traced around the embroidery fabric, within which the design would be completed. After embroidering, the excess fabric is trimmed away from the edge.

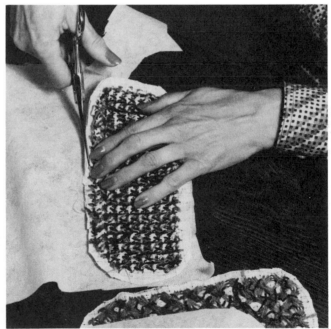

Iron-on Pellon, the kind used for interfacing (it can be medium weight or heavy duty) is cut to the precise size of each side of the case.

The Pellon is ironed onto the back side of each piece. Not only does the Pellon act as an interfacing, providing some stiffening, but it also reinforces the stitches and helps prevent snagging.

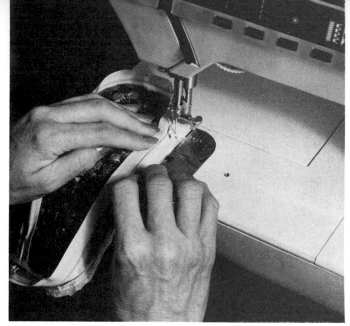

A soft, pliable zipper is sewn around one side.

➡️

Edges of the zipper are clipped open so that it does not pull and bind as it turns the curves of the case. The second side is then sewn to the zipper.

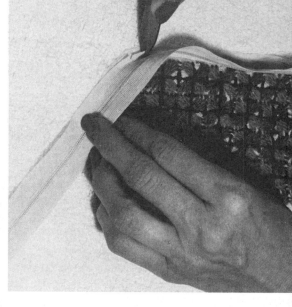

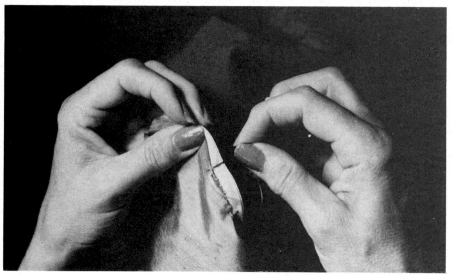

A lining is cut and hand-stitched to cover the zipper seam for one compartment; then the zipper is opened all the way and another piece of fabric is used to line that compartment.

In this case an edging is used, but the author did not like the effect and later removed it. This case effectively holds two to three pair of glasses when the zipper is opened all the way around. A more simple case can be made by lining each half of the case and stitching them together all around—just leaving an opening at the top into which to slip the glasses.

Another method, shown here, is to sew a zipper all around the two embroidered sides and then hand-stitch the lining in place. This kind of eyeglass case can accommodate up to three pair of glasses (if the size is large enough).

There are also many inventive ways of creating shopping bags or purses, using the same concepts as used with the eyeglass case; one is described here.

Making a Purse

Excess fabric is trimmed after the pattern is traced onto the piece—making certain to center the embroidery. (For the beginnings see p. 58 and pages 182–83.)

Fabric is cut for an interfacing (the kind used to line collars and shoulders in jackets), as well as a lining. The outer fabric is linen, and the lining is handwoven Thai silk in an orange color that picks up the colors of the flower.

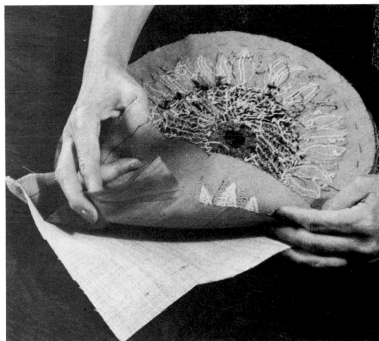

The right side of the lining is facing the right side of the embroidery, and interfacing is placed over the lining. All three parts are basted together.

The completed purse shown front and back.

Front

Mounting an Insert in a Book

The embroidery is pressed with a steam iron between two soft towels in order to avoid compressing the stitches. Any stretching to adjust angles and edges is accomplished at this point. For the beginnings see pages 69 and 70.

The stiffener, a piece of foam-core board that is supplied with the book, is placed behind the embroidery so that the piece is centered. It is then taped in place behind the board temporarily.

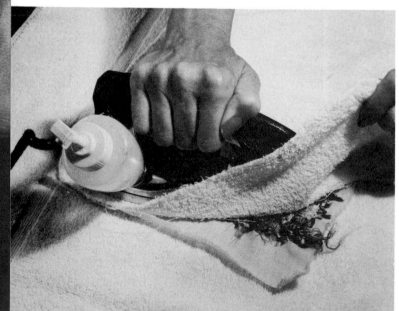

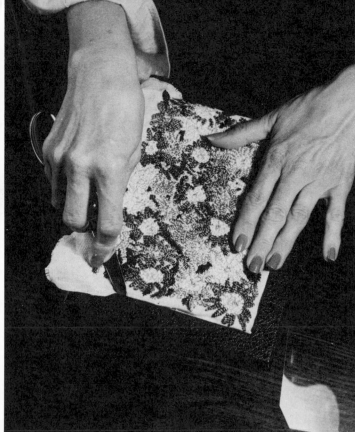

With the edge of a dull knife or scissors, the embroidery is slipped between the frame and back of the book until all parts are inserted and no loose edges are visible.

A piece of protective plastic (acetate) is inserted.

The completed book with anemone flowers worked in the long-legged cross-stitch.

ABOUT EMBROIDERED CLOTHING

Clothing can be embroidered before stitching parts together or can be embroidered after the garment is completed. Matching of embroidered parts may become a consideration if you embroider parts rather than the whole.

The ponchos shown at different points in this book are quite simple to make. The pattern is illustrated on pages 189 and 190.

(Many pattern companies sell specific patterns for embroidered pieces. They are usually pictured at the back of the pattern book.)

Making a Leather Photo Album from Scratch

Lee Newman's adaptation of a mola to canvas (14 squares to the inch) using a diagonal cross-stitch (gros point). (For the beginnings see p. 48.)

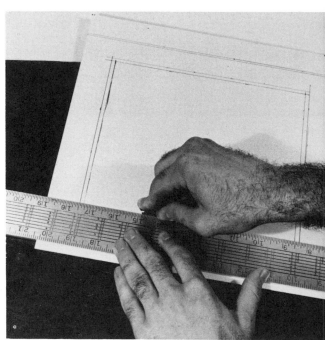

To make a leather photograph album with an embroidery framed on the cover, begin by constructing a cardboard template for each cover. Here, a window, to frame the embroidery, is cut from the cover template with a single-edge razor blade guided by a straightedge.

The cover template is tested by placing it over the mola embroidery. A fine smooth leather surface was desired for both the inside and the outside of both covers; therefore each cover is a double thickness of 3-ounce cowhide.

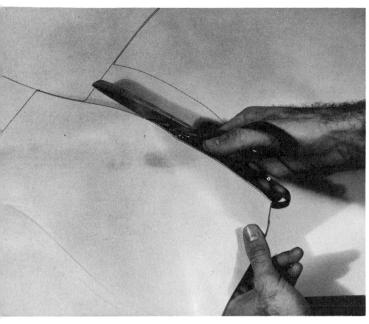

A total of four pieces are traced onto the cowhide and cut.

The window through which the embroidery will be seen is cut out with a razor knife after the outline has been traced from the template. Although it is difficult to cut an evenly beveled edge with a knife, it is possible. A mat cutter may also be used.

To enable the cover to fold open easily a small U-shaped channel is gouged out with a special tool—shown here. Or a knife may be used to create a V-shaped channel. The leather is then bent back to secure the crease before the leather is treated further.

In preparation for dyeing the leather, it should be cleaned of all grease and stains with saddle soap and water. Do not soak the leather, however. A gentle but thorough saddle soaping will help the dye to be absorbed evenly.

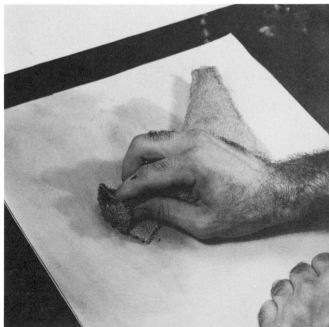

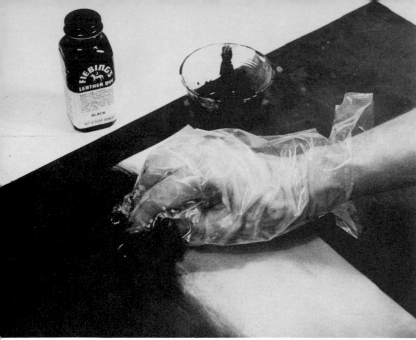

Fiebing's dye is applied with a soft cloth. Use a circular, continuous massaging motion all over the leather. Allow to dry for a few minutes, and then you may apply a second coat of dye.

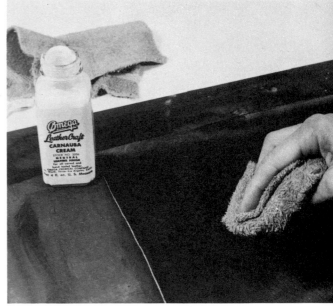

Apply a light coat of carnauba wax after the dye has dried. This will protect the dye during the gluing stages.

To laminate the front and back halves of the back cover, spread an even coat of Barge cement (or other leather cement) on each surface. Allow the Barge to almost dry. Then align the two pieces of leather (which should be identical in size), and press them together.

Start at one corner and carefully press one to the other, making certain that there are no air pockets, wrinkles, or bulges.

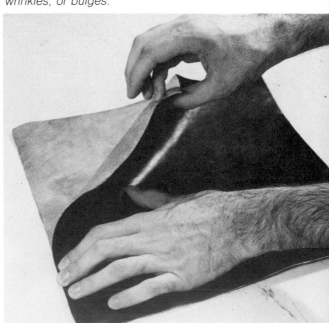

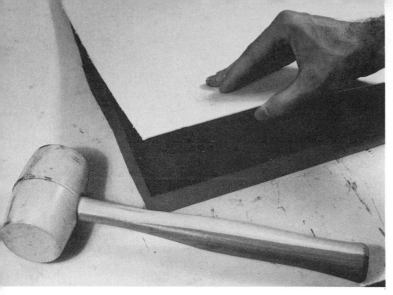

The cover should then be placed between pieces of cardboard and pounded—through the cardboard—with a rubber mallet to guarantee a strong adhesive bond. The cardboard protects the leather during this process. After pounding, the edges should be trimmed, if necessary, touched up with dye, and all edges and surfaces should be waxed.

The front cover is constructed in nearly the same fashion—except that the embroidery must be inserted. The embroidery is placed onto the bottom surface of the front cover after the Barge cement has almost dried. It must be carefully centered so that the top part—with the window—overlaps only a small portion of design.

The top portion of the front cover is then carefully pressed onto the bottom.

The front cover is then stitched around the window to secure both leather and embroidery.

The front cover should be carefully pounded (preferably between pieces of cardboard) to avoid any damage to the embroidery.

Holes are punched into the edge of the covers to accommodate metal posts, which will hold the covers and the album pages (available at stationers) together.

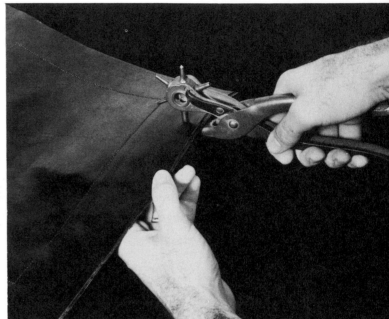

The completed album with embroidery insert on the front cover, by Lee Newman.

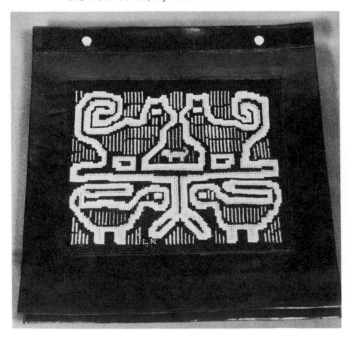

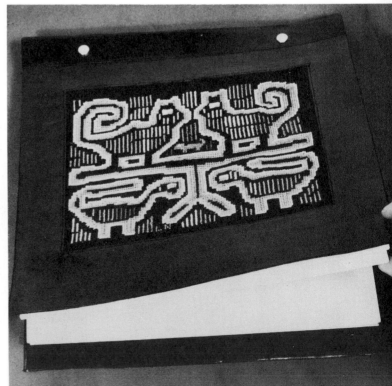

Bibliography

Chandler, Barbara. *Step-by-Step Guide to Embroidery*. London: Hamlyn Publishing Group, Ltd., 1973.

Dressmann, Cecile. *Embroidery*. New York: The Macmillan Company, 1971.

Editions Th. de Dillmont. *Morocco Embroideries*. Mulhouse, France: DMC Library, 1974.

Enthoven, Jacqueline. *The Stitches of Creative Embroidery*. New York: Van Nostrand Reinhold Company, 1964.

Fraser, B. Kay. *Modern Stitchery*. New York: Crown Publishers, Inc., 1976.

Gostelow, Mary. *A World of Embroidery*. New York: Charles Scribner's Sons, 1975.

Harbeson, Georgiana Brown. *American Needlework*. New York: Coward-McCann, Inc., 1938.

Haraszty, Eszter, and Cohen, Bruce David. *Needlepainting*. New York: Liveright, 1974.

Illes, Robert E. *Men in Stitches*. New York: Van Nostrand Reinhold Company, 1975.

Ireys, Katharine. *The Encyclopedia of Canvas Embroidery Stitch Patterns*. New York: Thomas Y. Crowell Company, 1972.

Johnston, Pauline. *A Guide to Greek Island Embroidery*. London: Victoria & Albert Museum, 1972.

Jones, Mary Eirwen. *A History of Western Embroidery*. New York: Watson-Guptill Publications, 1969.

Karasz, Mariska. *Adventures in Stitches*. Funk & Wagnalls, 1959.

Katzenberg, Gloria. *Needlepoint and Pattern*. New York: Macmillan Publishing Co., Inc., 1974.

Kroncke, Grete. *Mounting Handicraft*. New York: Van Nostrand Reinhold Company, 1967.

Orr, Jan. *Now Needlepoint*. New York: Van Nostrand Reinhold Company, 1975.

Paige-Burns, Hidley, and Thorne-Thompson, Kathleen. *American Cross-Stitch*. New York: Van Nostrand Reinhold Company, 1974.

Snook, Barbara. *The Creative Art of Embroidery*. London: Hamlyn Publishing Group, Ltd., 1972.

Thompson, Ginnie. *Teach Yourself Counted Cross-Stitch*. Libertyville, Ill: Leisure Arts, Inc., 1975.

Wilson, Erica. *Erica Wilson's Embroidery Book*. New York: Charles Schribner's Sons, 1973.

Supply Sources

Almost every village, town, and city has one or more needlework suppliers. Most five-and-tens sell basic supplies. These shops can be located in the telephone directory. For those who live away from sources, there are some good mail-order suppliers. A few are listed here.

General Supplies

A Touch of Class   Needlework supplies
12506 Memorial Drive
Houston, Tex. 77024

Alice Peterson   Needlework supplies
207 E. Franklin
El Segundo, Calif. 90245

American Crewel & Canvas Studio   Needlework supplies
P. O. Box 298
Boonton, N.J. 07005

Binney & Smith, Inc.
380 Madison Ave.
New York, N.Y. 10017

Crayola fabric
Crayons

Chaparral
2505 River Oaks Blvd.
Houston, Tex. 77019

Complete line of needlework materials including Paternayan, Appleton, Knox Linen, Anchor Linen, Marlitt & Ostara rayon, DMC, Pearsalls & Zwicky silk, etc.

Charles Craft, Inc.
P. O. Box 1169
Laurinburg, N.C. 28352

Counted cross-stitch fabrics including Hardanger 22 and Aida 11 and 14 in bolts, rolls, or cut pieces

Designer Arts
P. O. Box 463
Vandalia, Ohio 45377

Accessories and needlework supplies

Handwork Bazaar
3839 Richmond Ave.
Houston, Tex. 77027

Needlework supplies

J. L. Hammett Co.
Weaving and Fibers Division
10 Hammett Place
Braintree, Mass. 02184

Complete needlework supplies

Joan Toggett Ltd.
246 Fifth Ave.
New York, N.Y. 10001

One of the most complete lines of fabrics, threads, accessories, canvases, kits, magazines, and books

Mary McGregor
P. O. Box 154
Englewood, Ohio 45322

Paternayan Persian yarns and other needlework accessories

Schole House for the Needle
1206 Jamestown Rd.
Williamsburg, Va. 23185

Needlework supplies, particularly even-weave fabrics

The Hammock Shop
P. O. Box 308
Pawleys Island, S.C. 29585

Full line of needlework supplies and Ginnie Thompson designs

The Threaded Needle
1620 Massachusetts Ave.
Lexington, Mass. 02173

Complete needlework supplies

Unicorn, Inc.
Champaign, Ill. 61820

Fabuprint—iron-on design paper in colors

Windsor Button Shop
36 Chauncey St.
Boston, Mass. 02111

A chain of shops carrying a very complete line of needlework materials

In Great Britain

Harrods, Ltd.
Brompton Rd.
London SW 1, England

Complete needlework supplies

The Ladies' Work Society, Ltd.
138 Brompton Rd.
London SW 3, England

Complete needlework supplies
Appleton yarns

The Needlewoman Shop
146 Regent St.
London W1, England

Complete needlework supplies including Goldfingering and Appleton yarns

The Royal School of Needlework
25 Princes Gate
S. Kensington
London SW 7, England

Complete needlework supplies including instruction

Accessories

A Touch of Class
12506 Memorial Drive
Houston, Tex. 77024

Needle threader

Aqua Survey & Instrument Co., Inc.
7041 Vine St.
Cincinnati, Ohio 45216

Pendant lamp worn around neck to light needlework

Boye Needle Co.
916 Arcade
Freeport, Ill. 61032

Needles

Coats & Clark Sales Corp.
430 Park Ave.
New York, N.Y. 10022

Polyweb iron-on fusing tape and interfacings

Craft Accessories
P. O. Box 1261
Midland, Mich. 48640

Accessories for needlework including magnifier lamp with fluorescent light

Eberhard Faber Inc.
Crestwood
Wilkes-Barre, Pa. 18703

Needlecraft markers

Needle-Ease
81 Uplands Drive
West Hartford, Conn. 06107

Floor frame stands

Needlegraph
P. O. Box 186
Huntington Station
Dix Hills, N.Y. 11746

Black-lined reproducible graph paper

Penn Products
963 Newark Ave.
Elizabeth, N.J. 07207

Embroidery hoops

Sanford Corp.
2740 Washington Blvd.
Bellwood, Ill. 60104

NĒPO markers

Sangray Corp.
2318 Lakeview
P. O. Box 2388
Pueblo, Colo. 81004

Fabulon iron-on transfer for any printed images

Sewing Notions Division
Scovill Manufacturing Co.
Dept. 5524
Spartanburg, S.C. 29301

Dritz tracing paper, tracing wheels

Walker Distributors
P. O. Box 140011
Dallas, Tex. 75214

Maggie Pearce yarn threader

Kits and Patterns

Cross Stitchery
301 Xavier
Garland, Tex. 75043

Counted cross-stitch kits

Dover Needlework Books
Dover Publications, Inc.
180 Varick St.
New York, N.Y. 10014

Many books containing design resources

Folkwear Ethnic Patterns
Box 98
Foustville, Calif. 95436

Patterns for clothing with ethnic patterns

Ginnie Thompson Originals
Box 825
Pawleys Island, S.C. 29585

Cross-stitch kits

Happyendings   Tennis racquet covers
1110 North Drive
St. Louis, Mo. 63122

June Dole—Cross-stitch Kits   Counted cross-stitch kits
1280 North Stone Street
West Suffield, Conn. 06093

Wrights Needlework   Needlepoint kits trimmed with leather
West Warren, Mass. 01092

Computer Printouts

The Computer Place   Open all year
California State Museum of Sci-
   ence and Industry
700 State Drive
Los Angeles, Calif. 90037

The Computer Place   Open all year
Underground Atlanta
43-B Kenney's Alley
Atlanta, Ga. 30303

The Computer Place   Open all year
Omni International Bazaar
Omni International
Atlanta, Ga. 30303

Portraits by Computer   Open all year
Chicago Museum of Science and
   Industry
57th St. and Lakeshore Dr.
Chicago, Ill. 60637

The Computer Place   Open May–December
Van Buren St.
P. O. Box 669
Nashville, Ind. 47448

The Computer Place   April–November
Six Flags Over Mid-America
P. O. Box 666
Eureka, Mo. 63205

The Computer Place   All year
Crown Center Ships #WV-146
2450 Grand Ave.
Kansas City, Mo. 64108

Portraits by Computer
The Franklin Institute
20th and Parkway—1st Floor
   Museum
Philadelphia, Pa. 19103

Open all year

The Computer Place
New Market, Head House Square
2nd and Pine Sts.
Philadelphia, Pa. 19147

Open all year

The Computer Place
Six Flags Over Texas
2201 Road to Six Flags
Arlington, Tex. 76010

April–November

The Computer Place
C.N. Tower
301 Front St., W
Toronto, Ontario, Canada

Open all year

The Computer Place
Manitoba Museum of Man and
   Nature
190 Rupert Ave.
Winnipeg, Manitoba, Canada R3B
   ON2

Open all year

Threads and Yarns

Belding Lily Co.
P. O. Box B
Shelby, N.C. 28150

Lily yarns and threads—full range of thread,
cotton, rayon, wool, silk, in beautiful colors

Bernat & Sons Inc.
Uxbridge, Mass. 01569

Wool needlework yarns

Coats & Clark
75 Rockefeller Plaza
New York, N.Y. 10019

Wool, rayon, cotton, silk

DMC Corp.
107 Trumbull
Elizabeth, N.J. 07206

Wool and cotton—full range of colors

Paternayan Bros.
312 East 95th St.
New York, N.Y. 10028

Wool needlework yarns

Mounters

Adolph Burkland & Sons, Inc.
28-18 Steinway St.
Long Island City, N.Y. 11103

Book covers, boxes, frames

Art Bag Creations, Inc.
735 Madison Ave.
New York, N.Y. 10021

Handbags and tote bags

Modern Needlepoint Mounting
11 W. 32nd St.
New York, N.Y. 10001

Handbags, tote bags, belts, eyeglass cases, tennis racquet covers, picture frames, etc.

Nicholas Oberle, Inc.
558 Madison Ave.
New York, N.Y. 10022

Shoe and slipper mounting

Index